Endorsements

"People come into your life and sometimes you are not sure why. At least at first. To learn about Katie's journey, escaping the oppressive Communists from her native Laos, seeing her family broken apart, coming to the US, and having to start over, even having to learn a new language, is a journey that would break many. Katie's story is instead one of hope, joy, and finding and living a life of great faith. This is a story that will uplift you, that will remind you that, through faith, anything is possible. This is a book that will lift your heart."

Chuck Wright
Commissioner, Texas Veterans Commission

"Katie's story is like a healing balm, crossing generations, giving unexpected hope to the most tragic events. Her candor is refreshing, and her faith is deeply inspiring! If you're seeking hope and are burned out on religion, you'll find a mentor and friend in Katie's book."

Me Ra Koh
CEO of Fiora

"This book is a powerful reminder that growth often begins where comfort ends. With a heartfelt story and practical wisdom, it challenges readers to reflect, reframe, and rise. Whether you're facing a personal setback or seeking purpose, this book offers clarity and motivation. A must-read for anyone ready to take bold steps toward a more meaningful life."

Jessica Bartnick
Co-Founder and CEO
Foundation for C.H.O.I.C.E. & The Beauty Hub

"This compelling story will not only bring you to tears, but straight to the feet of Jesus. No matter where your life has brought you or what it has taught you, God has been pursuing you, He's been in control, and He has a plan. Katie's faith and desire to grow as a believer is infectious. This read will leave you hungry in your own pursuit of Him."

Jen Mango
aka The Happy Mango
Gifter, Decorator, Speaker, and Author of *Rescued Heart,*
Moving from Pain to Purpose

"Lasoy takes us on an unimaginable journey from hopelessness to transformation, redemption, and joy! Lasoy uses engaging storytelling and vivid language to convey her innermost and deepest feelings. There are so many golden nuggets throughout this book to keep you sitting on the edge of your seat wanting more! As you're drawn into this raw and intense life story, apply these lessons to your personal life. It discusses matters of setting boundaries, forgiveness, rejection and accepting the love of our heavenly Father. Allow this book to encourage you to go out into a hurting and broken world to be the hands and feet of Jesus Christ. Do not be ashamed or afraid to ask friends and neighbors about their personal relationship with Jesus. Do not just assume what people are going through based on the outside appearance. It is time to take a stand as true believers and change the world for the better."

Evelyn L. Brooks
Texas State Board of Education, District 14

"Katie's story is epic, incredible, and reads like a movie from beginning to end. This book will touch your life forever!"

Jill Hellwig
Founder, CEO, Head Coach, Brand New U, LLC
Author of *Grow With Goals* and *Go With Goals*

"As I turned the pages of a vibrant storybook chronicling a woman's journey from a challenging childhood to becoming a compassionate community leader, each word resonated deeply, moving me to tears with her remarkable strength and perseverance in her path toward faith. Her name is Lasoy, and Lasoy will inspire you to believe."

Angela A. Powell, MBA
CEO Powell Advantage, LLC
Former Elected Plano Independent School District
School Board Trustee, Place 2 (2017-2025)

"Gripping, emotional, inspirational. These words barely scratch the surface when describing the impact of Katie's journey. Enduring physical and emotional trauma which could easily crush a person's spirit, Katie's unconquerable will and her faith in God define what it means to "never give up." I highly recommend reading *The Journey of Redemption*."

Mike Mattocks
Senior Director Corporate Sponsorships
Dallas Mavericks

"Katie's book is a testimonial of how big our God is, and He wants a relationship with us! She was left without a mother, and her abusive father almost killed her, but God saved her to share this story of hope in Jesus with us. This story will change your life."

Jennifer Sheehan Elsaesser
Founder and President of HE is Hope

THE
Journey
OF
Redemption
FROM
East
to
West

LASOY KATIE
SINGLETON

The Journey of Redemption
From East to West
Lasoy Katie Singleton

To contact the author:
Katies@community75.org

Published by:

Mary Ethel

Mary Ethel Eckard
Frisco, Texas

Library of Congress Control Number: 2025907539
ISBN (Print): 978-1-966561-13-2
ISBN (E-book): 978-1-966561-14-9

"You can't heal the people you love;
you can't make choices for them; you
can't rescue them. However,
you can promise that they won't journey alone.
You can loan them your map, but this trip is theirs."
~ Laura Jean Truman

CONTENTS

Dedication xi

Acknowledgments xiii

Introduction xvii

SECTION 1: SABAI DEE MAI

Chapter 1   Forged in War 1

Chapter 2   Kindness in Darkness 17

SECTION 2: GUTTED

Chapter 3   East Meets West 25

Chapter 4   Taye Soup and Soy Beans 31

Chapter 5   Hide and Seek 37

Chapter 6   Ducklings 43

Chapter 7   Elusive Mother Figure 49

Chapter 8   Erased In the Attic 59

Chapter 9   In The Name of Acceptance 65

SECTION 3: Y'ALL

Chapter 10   The Dating Scene...73

Chapter 11   U-Turn to Texas... 81

Chapter 12   Seasons and Realities..................................... 91

Chapter 13   Why Not You? 99

Chapter 14   Pursued by God... 107

SECTION 4: KINTSUGI

Chapter 15   Lasoy Coming up for Air........................... 117

Chapter 16   Washed and Redeemed 125

Chapter 17   Don't Ride That Sail.................................. 131

Chapter 18   Deeper joy 139

Conclusion.. 147

About the Author 153

DEDICATION

To God, whose love, protection, and guidance have illuminated my path and inspired every word within these pages.

To my beloved husband, Van, whose steadfast support and encouragement have been my anchor through this journey, showing me what unconditional love looks like. Through hard times, good times, and the times in between, we are each other's partners. Here's to many more adVANtures.

To our wonderful children, Kohl, Patrick, and Isabella, whose laughter and love fill my life with joy and purpose.

To my sister, Bounmy, whom I look up to as my mother, sister, and friend. Thank you for your love, support, and sacrifice to push forward against all odds.

To my dear friends, whose belief in me and unwavering support have been invaluable throughout the writing of this book.

This journey of redemption is a testament to God's faithfulness, mercy, love, and strength.

Thank you for being a part of my story.

ACKNOWLEDGMENTS

Thank you to my friend, Jill Hellwig, who encouraged me in my walk of faith. She is my Barnabus, always joyful and encouraging. This book would not have happened without her support and wisdom.

Throughout life, when I shared my experience of coming to America, many people would tell me I needed to write a book. However, the pain of putting anything on paper was too heavy. I first needed to heal through God's words and for Him to bring the right encourager to help me write His story about my life to share my testimony. God partners all of us for His purpose and in His timing. Jill was His partner for me.

"But now thus saith the Lord that created thee, O Jacob, and He that formed thee, O Israel, fear not: for I have redeemed thee, I have called thee by thy name, thou art mine. When thou passest through the waters, I will be with thee; and through the rivers, they shall not overflow thee; when thou walkest through the fire, thou shalt not be burned; neither shall the flame kindle upon thee."

~ Isaiah 43:1-2

INTRODUCTION

The morning after my baptism, while finishing my makeup and hair routine, my hand brushed across a scar on my upper right eyebrow. In elementary school, a boy had thrown a rock at me, and it tore open my forehead. As I applied lipstick, I could feel the tip sink into another scar left by a dog attack on my thirteenth birthday. As though a light had been turned on, something looked different about my appearance.

For years, I was crippled by the memories of those scars. They were painful reminders of rejection the enemy, Satan, had whispered; lies I believed for nearly forty-eight years. But on this particular morning, after my baptism and the strength it gave me, as the light caught the scars just right, I paused to look at them no longer with fear, hurt, or shame. Instead, I embraced them as an affirmation of the peace and truth that God has given me. He washed away the lies the enemy has used on all of us in beliefs about our beauty. It was as though I was seeing the scars from a new perspective. Staring into the mirror, this time with clarity, beauty, and renewed purpose, memories from long ago flashed back to what God had redeemed and restored. He brought beauty to my scars.

To fully share my testimony and struggle of having an intimate relationship with God, I must revisit my life before God, my life with God, and how God took what was broken and mended it, making it for His purpose. For some, God may be a pseudo figure to pray to and ask for things to happen. Perhaps those things came true and perhaps they didn't.

My pain was real, and the scars that riddled my body served as a daily reminder of losing my family and being raised by my sister. I didn't want anything to do with God. However, He wanted everything to do with me. My story of redemption would come through deep sorrow and bring me out with deeper joy. God was real in every sense because my pain was and is real. If someone could allow that much pain and sorrow, He must be real. Else, my life and what I have lost would be a figment of my imagination.

To this day, my relationship with God is intimate, and our conversations are personal, intended to heal the damage inflicted by lies from the enemy, which has not been easy. It aches me to the core to see how I was born during wartime yet causes me to stand tall in faith to see the beauty of my life today.

For those going through their own battles, know that God hears your prayers and sees your tears; not one of them is wasted. Just hold on. The God of Abraham is for you. He is in the smallest of detail to the biggest in your life.

My story is not to recruit you or persuade your faith, or lack thereof. That is for God to do. I hope to inspire you to know you are not defined by your darkest days, scars, or where you came from. It is from Whom you truly belong that gives you the strength to hold on in finding your place and peace amid life's chaos.

As you read further, my story may expose raw emotions and tears you have suppressed. May your tears be ones of hope and joy, not despair and pity. May the frustrations you feel raise up the warrior within you to help conquer your fears. For those struggling with the concept of faith or a relationship with God, know this. He is patiently waiting for you when YOU are ready. He is a God of grace, mercy, and redemption.

When God called me to share my testimony, I was not ready. In all honesty, I was angry with Him. Despite my resistance, His mercy and grace gave me the time to heal and the courage to press forward. Writing a book detailing the hardships, brokenness, and flaws I have overcome was the last thing I wanted to do. Below is my conversation with God when He asked me to help build His kingdom.

> *"Lord, where were you during all those times when I was left for dead, broken, beaten, and abandoned by those who were supposed to love and protect me? You could have used me during all those broken moments, but instead, I felt rejected and*

abandoned by you. All for what? To help build a kingdom for those who didn't want me? For those who made fun of my name? For those who betrayed my trust? For those who left me wounded and riddled me with scars? For those who said they were my sisters and friends only to use my insecurities against me?

"There are a million great Christians. Jesus-loving, Bible-thumping, holy roller Christians who would gladly write Your book. My family tree has been cut down to only five of us left on earth. I have nothing to offer, I am nobody! Why bring up my pain for others to pour salt on and reopen those wounds from so long ago? Why expose myself when my life is finally good, where I can do all the things most people could only dream of? Why now and Why me?"

God answered back, *"Why not you?"*

I knew what I had to do.

One day God will call me home, as he did my mother. Perhaps leaving my redeemed journal will help our children know where they came from. May it serve as a compass and road map to help them navigate their storms and brokenness. Mostly, I long to find my way back to my mother, to feel her embrace, and see her face for the first time on the other side of heaven. While I cannot promise our children an easy life without pain, I can promise them they will not face their storms alone.

"You can't heal the people you love;
you can't make choices for them;
you can't rescue them.
However, You CAN promise that
they won't journey alone.
You can loan them your map, but this trip is theirs."
~ Laura Jean Truman

Sabai Dee Mai

(Hello in Thai)

"And do this, knowing the time, that now it is high time to awake out of sleep; for now, our salvation is nearer than when we first believed. The night is far spent, the day is at hand. Therefore, let us cast off the works of darkness and let us put on the armor of light. Let us walk properly, as in the day, not in revelry and drunkenness, not in lewdness and lust, not strife and envy. But put on the Lord Jesus Christ, and make no provision for the flesh, to fulfill its lusts."
-Romans 13:11-14 NKJV

chapter

1

FORGED IN WAR

During the Vietnam War, Thailand was an ally of the United States and supported South Vietnam against the communist North. This alignment put Thailand at odds with North Vietnam, which led to some military skirmishes along their borders and concerns about communist expansion. Thailand served as a key base for American military operations during the Vietnam War, significantly influencing the country's economy and social landscape. While Thailand was not directly involved in combat on its soil, it played a vital supporting role by allowing the US to use its territory for military operations against North Vietnam. In the 1970s, tensions escalated due to the rise of the Khmer Rouge in Cambodia and the spillover of conflict into Thailand

and Laos. Thailand was concerned about the influence of Vietnam in Cambodia and its support for the communist movements in the region. This led to military skirmishes along the border.

Thailand's worries escalated when communist North Vietnam launched large-scale overt and covert operations in South Vietnam and adjoining areas including Cambodia, Laos, and the hinterlands of Thailand. The rapid advancements of guerrillas and regular troops of North Vietnam exposed Thai frontiers. In 1961, the Communist Party of Thailand (CPT) revolted against the Thai government and began an armed struggle. Many other communist groups, emboldened by the rise of communism, fanned insurgency in the Northeastern provinces of Thailand.

Our father, Bounchan, was born in Thailand and joined the resistance army to help fight against the communist movement invading along the Northern borders. Later, he was sent to Laos to help fight against the Viet Cong and was trained by the American military. While in Laos our father met our mother, Dy, who was of Tai Dam descent. The original country of the Tai Dam was Sip Song Chau Tai or the Twelve Tai Principalities. In 1888, this ancient country was colonized and annexed to Tonkin of Vietnam by the French. In 1948, it was established as a semi-independent state called the Tai Federation under the rule of France. Since 1954, and under the Communist Vietnamese, it has completely lost its identity as a nation, absorbed into the northwestern region of Vietnam.

When the French and Tai forces were defeated by the Communist Vietnamese at Muong Theng (Dien Bien Phu) in 1954, the Tai administration and their families who opposed the communist insurgents were forced to flee to Laos and some to South Vietnam. Those who resettled in Laos lived there peacefully through 1975 and became known as Tai Dam.

In 1975, when the communists took over Laos, the Tai Dam fled to Thailand to seek asylum. From Thailand, 12,000 Tai Dam were resettled in France, Canada, Australia, and the United States.

Part of our mother's family settled alongside the Xian Khoang, Laos village. While our father was in Laos helping to drive out the Viet Cong during the uprising, our mother's village was bombed; they were collateral damage from the heavy bombing that took place in Xian Khoang.

One of the bombings was called *Operation Barrel Roll*. It was a covert interdiction and close air support campaign conducted in the Kingdom of Laos by the United States military between 5 March 1964 and 29 March 1973, concurrent with the Vietnam War. During the operation, U.S. Air Force 2nd Air Division and U.S. Navy Task Force 77 dropped 260 million bombs on Laos.

The operation was launched to persuade the Democratic Republic of Vietnam (North Vietnam) to stop supporting the insurgency in the Republic of Vietnam (South Vietnam). It became an interdiction campaign against North Vietnam's main logistical corridor, which ran from southwestern North Vietnam, through southeastern Laos, and into South Vietnam. The operation also increasingly provided close air support for the Royal Lao Armed Forces, CIA-backed tribal mercenaries, and Thai Volunteer Defense Corps in a covert ground war in northern and northeastern Laos. *Barrel Roll* and the "Secret Army" attempted to stem an increasing tide of the People's Army of Vietnam (PAVN) and Pathet Lao offensives.

Barrel Roll was one of the most closely held secrets of the American military commitment in Southeast Asia. Due to the ostensible neutrality of Laos, guaranteed by the Geneva Conference of 1954 and 1962, both the U.S. and North Vietnam strove to maintain the secrecy of their operations and only slowly escalated military actions there. In 1975, Laos emerged from nine years of war as devastated as any of the other Asian participants in the Vietnam War.

After the bombing took place in Laos, sadly, none of our mother's family survived except for her sister and herself. During the mass bombing, our father found her hidden, seeking shelter away from the communist soldiers. Later he would take her in to live with him. Soon after being rescued by our father, they had an arranged marriage. Perhaps she agreed to the marriage because there were no other options during the Vietnam war and the exchange of marrying a much older man for safety was the best choice she felt she had.

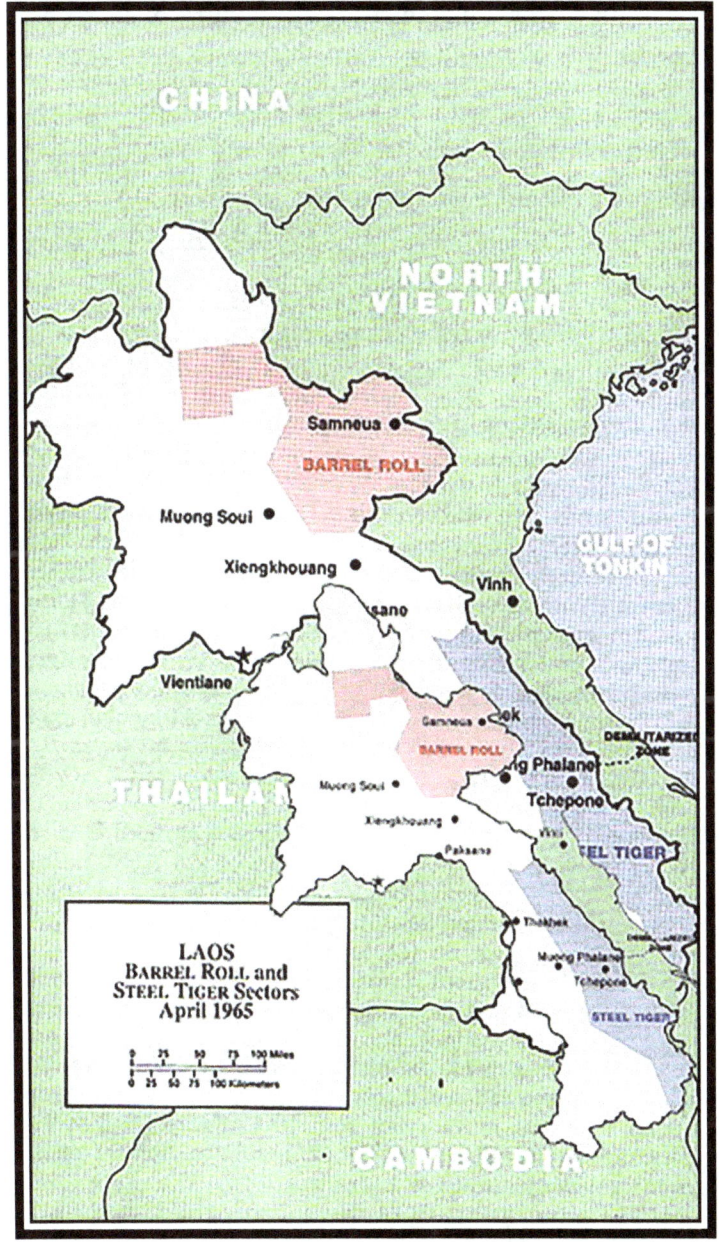

CHINA

NORTH VIETNAM

Samneua

BARREL ROLL

Muong Soui

Xiengkhouang

sano

Vinh

GULF OF TONKIN

Vientiane

Samneua   ek

BARREL ROLL

Muong Soui

Xiengkhouang

ng Phalane

DEMILITARIZED ZONE

Tchepone

THAILAI

Pakuane

EL TIGER

Thakhek

Muong Phalane

Tchepone

STEEL TIGER

LAOS
BARREL ROLL and
STEEL TIGER Sectors
April 1965

0   25   50   75   100 Miles
0   25   50   75   100 Kilometers

CAMBODIA

Our mother did not have the luxury of love and would tell my oldest sister, Bounmy, to make the most of what was given. I am the youngest of five, Bounmy the oldest, followed by my sister Ylene, brother Vec, and sister Taye. Our mother would emphasize the importance of education, being resourceful, and making the most of any situation. Like many Asians escaping the Vietnam War, our family was no different in enduring the cruelty that war ushers in by destroying lives. The reality is that war creates children raising children.

Our mother, Dy, was strong, loving, and wise for such a young age. Meanwhile, our father joined the guerrilla resistance movement to fight against the communist movement. Perhaps, seeing so much death and fighting in the army, he created demons of his own. His form of communication was to abuse and hit. He hit us during good times and during bad times. He would find anything lying around to beat us with. Perhaps the demons he tried to keep at bay were too hard to contain, and the only release was to take it out on us kids.

While my mother was pregnant with me, they would fight and he would kick her in the stomach, knocking her unconscious. Sadly, Bounmy, as a child, would recall the horrific injuries our mother endured while pregnant with me in the womb. She would remember the time our father pulled a gun and fired it between my mother's legs after beating her. It is a miracle she survived, and I was not harmed. After the gun incident, our father didn't come back home, which I'm sure was a welcome relief for our mother.

Shortly after that, Southeast Asia countries such as Laos, Vietnam, and Cambodia, took a turn for the worst. The communist movement started moving closer along the northern border of Thailand and Laos. In many countries, the communist movement did not come in the middle of the night to take away people's property. Instead, they pushed propaganda of "for the betterment of the people" businesses now belong to the "people." They used shame and guilt as a weapon to force people to comply. The utopia they promised was far from the reality they created.

Meanwhile, they bombed the first line of defense, such as the local police, and targeted the youth, promising freedom with a life of luxury with free education and safety for their compliance. They pit the youth against their families, telling them they, the Communist Party, knew better while tearing down temples and taking away any form of God. When the communist movement came in, they burned down buildings, drove out educators and doctors, and there was little infrastructure left. They made daily life a living hell.

While my mother was pregnant with me, she gathered what she could to escape with my siblings, knowing the horrible living situation that was to come if we stayed. To pay for our expenses along the way, she hid jewelry sewn in her clothing, smuggling them out before soldiers could raid our house. She heard there was safety in Thailand, where America was going to be setting up refugee camps near the border of Thailand in Nong Khai. We made our way toward Nong Khai, Thailand, out of Laos. During the trek from Laos to Thailand, the harshness of traveling while caring for us may have taken its toll on our mother. We settled in a village near Vang Vieng, a small town north of Vientiane, on the Nam Song River in Laos, surrounded by striking limestone mountains and caves. After days of complaining of painful stomach issues, and screaming out loud, sadly, it was too much for her to endure. She passed away five months after giving birth to me. Bounmy did not know the exact complications she passed away from but did know it was sometime in the early morning. On the official US documents coming to America, her cause of death was listed as "stomach issues." It could have been multiple things, but the biggest was not having doctors and a hospital nearby.

At her death bed, she made Bounmy promise to keep the family together, to not separate us, and to keep a close eye on me. I cannot imagine how heavy the weight of that promise must have been for Bounmy to carry. She was just a child herself and carrying such a heavy burden is hard to imagine. At the age of nearly 10, she became my mother, father, and sister. I cry thinking of her lost childhood and the sacrifice she made to keep our mother's promise.

Though I would never see our mother's face, know what she looked like, or hear her voice, I knew I was loved and wanted by her. While in the process of writing this book, I've been able to discover the full richness of our heritage, especially on our mother's side, our people, the Tai Dam. I feel like I've been awakened from a slumber regarding our heritage.

Our mother paid the ultimate price trying to get us to America. She wanted to give us an opportunity to have a better life, to live out the dream she was denied, and to have the luxury of finding love of our own choice.

Though I would never see our mother's face, know what she looked like, or hear her voice, I knew I was loved and wanted by her.

As I've gotten older, I still long to know our mother, feel her embrace, what she may have looked like, and hear her stories and advice. But most of all, I wish she were alive so Bounmy would not have to bear such heavy responsibility of that promise, and for Bounmy to have a childhood of her own.

However, that was not the card we were dealt, and, like our dying mother said, we would have to make the most of the situation and what little that was given to us.

The Journey to Thailand

After the death of our mother, our father didn't come back for us, perhaps he was sent off on another military mission. Either way, he left us abandoned and parentless.

Bounmy took it hard, but there was no time to dwell on our mother's death or why our father did not return. We were in the midst of war, and safety was our main concern. People in the village told her that help was coming, but she knew better. "Help" would usually come in the form of communist propaganda, which led to re-education camps where children would not come back. If they did, they were brainwashed, and some were forced to kill their own families for the "greater good."

Seeing us without parents, other families in the village wanted to help, but they could either take only me as a baby or separate us. Bounmy was adamant that it was all of us or nothing. Those were dark times for everyone, as they were trying to escape for a better life themselves. Taking on all five of us was difficult for most families. However, Bounmy knew she would have to search for inner strength if we were to survive. She would have to rely on her faith rooted in God and trust Him for provision.

After realizing our father may not come back and the "help" that was to come either meant death or separation, Bounmy snuck us out of the village to continue the trek toward safety at the American refugee camps she heard of in Thailand or perhaps find family on our father's side in Thailand. With only an orange soda and a handful of food, she recalled a voice guiding her. She would carry me in a sling on her back or her frontside like most mothers carried their infant child. Similar to a kangaroo with a pouch, I was her baby joey. To make money and provide food for us, she lied about her age to find work. Life and times during that era were filled with sorrow and death where food was little to come by and seeing parentless children was sad, but not uncommon.

Working in the rice fields, Bounmy would carry me on her back, never complaining. She would do anything to protect us, even skip her meals to ensure we had enough. Surviving war meant anything was possible to make it out alive, like a child taking care of a five-month-old baby and three other siblings under age six. For many months, we went without a roof over our heads, where an eggplant would have to be stretched and shared among the five of us. Hunger and fear were a daily part of life.

It's impossible to think how we survived without getting caught by communist soldiers. Bounmy would tell me it was because God and our mother were watching over us from heaven, and my mother would come down at night to breastfeed me and rock me to sleep. She said that's why I was so quiet and such a good baby when there was no milk for me, surviving only on a bottle of orange soda. Whether true or not, I would never take that thought away from Bounmy; her faith was all she had to help with our survival against all odds.

During those days, we were malnourished, and hunger was part of our daily routine. We had to suppress hunger and not think about it so that we could survive the journey to the refugee camp. As we were making our way toward Thailand, soldiers were looking to capture or kill people; adding five children they could indoctrinate and brainwash to support their army would be ideal. Capturing five of us to be foot soldiers would be beneficial to their communist movement. Bounmy was well aware of this and took the longer and more dangerous paths in the woods to provide us with better cover, even though it meant finding food and work would be more difficult.

On one occasion, the communist soldiers were so close, she could hear their footsteps and voices nearby. Quickly, she gathered us to get off the road and hide so we would not be captured. To camouflage us from the soldier's sight, she buried us in mud, underneath leaves, and held me close to her chest. As the soldiers drew near, she could see them through a tiny opening underneath the leaves and smell their smoldering cigarettes. She closed her eyes and prayed to God. She later recounted how she could feel angels spread their wings to shelter us so we would remain hidden. She said our mother was rocking me to sleep so I would not cry and alert our location to the soldiers.

Without a doubt, the Lord heard her prayers that day and came to cover us with the angels' wings. That miracle would remind Bounmy in the future to never give up on her faith in Christ. God was in every detail that day. We were indeed hidden from the soldiers' sight but seen by God. He was and is our rightful Father, even though I would not come to accept what God did for us until much later in life.

My walk of faith and obedience, like Bounmy's, would be a journey filled with scars, both physically and internally. Perhaps God knew I needed to go through the pain, struggles, and abandonment, because I needed an authentic relationship, birthed out of sorrow and deep pain to gain wisdom, peace, and purpose from God. In other words, I was stubborn, and God was patient! He already knew the plans He had for me while He knitted me in my mother's womb. As stubborn as I am, He knew those deep wounds and scars would be a testimony to be used as a weapon of encouragement, hope, and faith, even when I did not.

That miracle would serve to remind Bounmy in the future to never give up on her faith in Christ.

We continued on our way to the refugee camp, stopping in villages to find work, food, and shelter. In one village, we found our father and discovered he had another wife there. We had no other choice except to stay with them and endure his cruelty.

Bounmy was watchful and protective of me like I was her child. In every sense, I was. It was as though she had a sixth sense not to leave me alone with our father. This was the moment in my life that was the beginning of my strained relationship with God. I felt rejected and the enemy whispered, planting seeds of rejection and survivor's guilt, of being born and being a burden to

Bounmy. The accuser would whisper that I was the cause of our mother's death because she died after giving me life. Sadly, I believed this lie and blamed myself for our mother's death.

While in that village with our father, Bounmy was hired to work at a store, but she was unable to take me with her. She asked our sister, Ylene, to keep an eye on me and to not leave me alone with our father. In that village, people lived in makeshift homes made from various materials. Our home was made from metal and wouldn't survive the building code in America. Bounmy was told by neighbors that I wanted to use the bathroom and, as toddlers do, I cried to communicate my need. Our father had demons of his own, perhaps on that day they were too hard to hold back, he picked up my tiny body and threw me against the metal wall that had a sharp edge sticking out. My body hit the wall as if I were a rag doll. My stomach landed against the sharp metal edge which cut me open. I fell on the ground, making a loud thud, and bled out.

I'm not sure what happened next, but our father, perhaps out of panic, shame, guilt, drunkenness, or all of the above, left my tiny unconscious body on the ground in my pool of blood and abandoned me once more. Hours later, Bounmy recalls hearing a voice telling her to get home immediately. When she arrived, she discovered my near lifeless body covered in blood, lying in my pool of blood on the ground, and she cried out in horror, trying to find our father. He was nowhere to be found.

She ran to the neighbors begging them for help. They took my limp body to the hospital and, after examining me, the doctors said there was nothing they could do to help me. I had bled out for too long and lost too much blood. Bounmy begged the doctors to do what they could; she pleaded for them to stitch me up. They must have taken pity on her and, alone in an empty room with my body lying on the operating table, tears streaming down her face, Bounmy gently caressed my cheeks, holding my small hand, and prayed to God to bring me back to her. In that lonely room with my sister beside me, God once again heard her prayers and preserved my life. This is where I struggled with God.

I don't remember much about that day or event. I don't know what triggered our father's wrath to pick me up and throw me across the room. But I do know what I felt inside. I felt rejected by God. While I'm blessed to be alive today, at that time I didn't understand why God would bring me back to be a burden to my sister. In every sense, I felt rejected and sad while other people would have been happy to be alive.

I did not know the enemy had planted seeds of survivor's guilt and being a burden, blaming myself for our mother's death. That weight was so heavy. As a child, I couldn't process things that were not my fault, so I simply internalized things, making them my fault, regardless of whether it was true or false. I would tell myself that if I had not been born, our mother would still be alive, and my sister would have had her childhood. She wouldn't have another mouth to feed, and life would have been much better for them without me.

That seed was the beginning of my crutch. That lie filled me with so much sorrow that, at times, I could barely catch my breath, and my chest tightened with tears. Some days it would come out of nowhere. Many nights I would grieve, not sure where the pain came from. When I would fail or mess up, the accuser would whisper, "See, God didn't want you. Your mom died because of you, and now you're just a burden."

I believed every word, down to my core, making it hard to breathe at times. I would cry, not knowing where it came from. The shame and guilt were incredibly hard to escape. I cry for that little girl when I think about being abandoned by my father. The man who was supposed to protect me inflicted the first outward scar on my stomach; a reminder of rejection.

chapter

2

KINDNESS IN DARKNESS

During the Vietnam era, the US military served as a safeguard for families trying to escape the war. They partnered with other organizations, including Christian missionaries. I remember bits and pieces, but mostly the feeling of chaos. We heard stories about large families who had both parents but did not make it out alive, so we were fortunate to have survived without parents.

After my recovery from being thrown against the wall and bleeding out, Bounmy courageously packed us up and, once again, we made our way toward Nong Khai, Thailand. After nearly two years, we were fortunate to arrive at the American refugee camp, where we stayed from 1975 to late 1979. It's only by the grace of God guiding my sister's steps and path that we made it safely. While waiting to be vetted, we were provided shelter, food, vaccinations, and schooling where we were taught English, among other things. There we were finally able to rest our heads. We didn't have to worry about finding our next meal. There were no more sounds of bullets going off or the fear of being captured.

Being a child without parents had one advantage, which was the ability to explore alone. The Christian missionaries would set up churches to spread the gospel to the locals. One day, my wandering landed me at a missionary church where God used the most unlikely person to plant another seed. In this church was a statue of Jesus on the cross and my body froze as I stared at Jesus on the cross for the first time. Not knowing who He was, I could see this pain-filled body on the cross of someone hurt and bleeding. Without realizing how far I had wandered from Bounmy, I couldn't find her and, panicking, started to cry. I looked frantically for my sister, but she was nowhere to be found. I felt alone and scared, thinking the communist soldiers were nearby and would capture me.

At that moment, an American soldier found me. I don't remember his face, but I felt his kindness during a time when kindness was hard to find. I was frightened, and this American soldier found me and reached for my hand. I'm not sure why I took his hand because, during our trek, Bounmy was protective and warned us that strangers were not to be trusted. But that day, I trusted this stranger who saw me. As I reached to take his hand, he knelt down and softly said, "That is our Lord and Savior, Jesus Christ."

Immediately my fears subsided and were replaced with wonderment. I wouldn't realize the full impact of his words or the importance of that day until later. Looking back, I barely spoke Thai, and I'm not even sure how I understood his words, but I knew what he said and how it made me feel.

> As I reached to take his hand, he knelt down and softly said, "That is our Lord and Savior, Jesus Christ."

I will always be indebted to our military for rescuing my family and keeping us alive. I am eternally grateful for the overwhelming kindness of that soldier, who may never know the impact he made on a little girl's life. That was such a beautiful moment when every other day was filled with darkness, hunger, and sadness, and for a brief moment, it all went away. Maybe God knew my internal battle with the enemy's whisper and He, too, planted the seed of hope in Jesus to combat the whispers and wait for me to discover Him.

Safely back with Bounmy, the long journey of being vetted continued. During that process, we came to realize the cruelty of communism. Bounmy needed to be eighteen to sign sponsorship papers to get us out of the Thai refugee camp so we could be sent to a different country. That meant she had to search for any surviving family members to keep the promise to our mother. Sadly, she discovered that none of our mother's side of the family survived after the bombing, and she couldn't find the rest of our family on our father's side. (Years later we would discover our mother did have one sister who survived the bombing and there were some surviving family members on our father's side in Thailand.) At the refugee camp, the reality set in that perhaps none of our family members survived. There was hope that maybe our father made it out alive.

Bounmy decided it didn't matter which country or where we went, as long as we remained a unit. As horrible as our father was, she knew the only way to get us out of a horrible wartime situation was to pray for our father's return. Just like the end of a basketball game with five seconds left on the clock, our father arrived close to the cutoff time to sign the paperwork for us to get out of the Nong Khai refugee camp. Perhaps, because our father served in the military, and helped the American army, he had the special privilege of expediting our approval process to be sponsored in America and to be part of the first wave of refugees to come to the States in the 1970s. We don't know how or why our dad agreed to sign the paperwork because, to him, being in Thailand was much better than being in America. In Thailand, he could be the top dog in the chain of culture hierarchies. He would forever torment Bounmy about coming to America. Either way, I didn't care for the reason he signed it; he did and that was good enough for me.

We were blessed to receive the good news that a British family living in Washington State had agreed to sponsor our family. We were nervous about our new lives and what waited for us, but anything would be better than what we left behind. Our mother dreamed that we find a better life in America, make the most of what was given to us, and perhaps achieve the American dream.

Though our mother and relatives did not make it out of the war alive, I believe their voices lived within us as we journeyed to America. The odds were stacked against us, but somehow, we made it as children raising children. It was God who guided the soldier when I was lost, standing in front of the cross. It was God who planted those words, "Jesus Christ, our Lord, and Savior," that I carried from Thailand to America when I could barely speak, let alone understand the soldier's English words as clear as day.

From that point, our journey from the East to the West began. Little did I know I had carried God's message deep inside, waiting to be discovered in time.

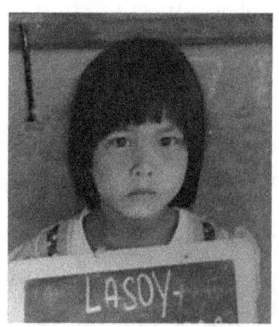

My picture was taken in the refugee camp
before heading to America

Gutted

(British term for very upset or disappointed)

"'For I know the thoughts that I think toward you,' saith the Lord,
'thoughts of peace, and not of evil, to give you an expected end.
Then shall ye call upon me, and ye shall go and pray unto me,
and I will hearken unto you.'"
-Jeremiah 29:11-12 NKJV

chapter

3

EAST MEETS WEST

The year was 1979, and since our father was a soldier helping to fight the Communist Party, we were granted to be among the first wave of immigrants voyaging to America by plane. Our father, his new wife, and their daughter, Noi, my half-sister, traveled with us. As I gazed out the airplane window on our journey to America, I was captivated by the clouds below, they were majestic, beautiful, full of colors like flowers, as though I could smell the freedom stored within their beauty. Our destination to America would be the Pacific Northwest of Washington State, a place that promised new beginnings. The scent of liberation was a welcome relief, a stark contrast to the fear of gunfire and capture that had haunted me.

One of my earliest memories of arriving in America

was an airline stewardess who gave me a pin with the wings of an airplane and a bag of Skittles, my first candy. I look back at the symbolism of those two items and it brings such deep meaning that, once again, God was in the smallest of details: wings and a bag of rainbow candy. Who would have thought? Sitting on the cold floor of the airport, looking for these strangers who would take us in as our sponsors, I felt a sense of nervousness and out of place as people walked by. Looking down at a small bag of sticky rice, which I held in one hand and a bag of Skittles in the other hand as a snack, I was aware I was at a crossroads of two cultures, unsure where I fit in. This would be a long road of self-discovery.

In the distance, figures came closer. These people were to be our British family and had agreed to sponsor our entire family, including our father and his "new" family. They arrived to take us home to begin our journey of assimilating into the American culture. Without them, we would not be in America, and we are grateful they agreed to be our sponsor. I'm sure they, too, were unsure what they had gotten themselves into. As part of the sponsorship program to help immigrants escape the Vietnam War, sponsors were given payment from the government to help cover the costs of taking in refugees, which helped get legal immigrants to America.

On the car ride to the sponsor family's house, I looked out the window and saw a different landscape with tall green trees, nice homes, and people going about their day.

I rolled down the window to take a deep breath of the new homeland. For the first time, I truly felt a sense of relief. Our sponsor family lived in a small town called Redondo Beach, Washington. They had a large family, and I came to have a closer connection with our sponsor mom, Ivy, and I looked to her as a mother figure. She was a wonderful British lady with red hair, almost like Lucille Ball, and she didn't have children of her own. She married a man, Lathe, who had two sons from his former marriage. They had adopted two other children, daughters, named Jezel and Cheryl. At that time, their children were much older, and some were already out of the house.

As we arrived, Ivy took us to the basement where we would stay. Looking around the big empty room, we unpacked what little we had in our bags. We weren't sure what to do. The first few nights, we slept close to each other with little more than one bag of our belongings combined. Those were both exciting and scary times, learning a new culture and language.

Ivy took the major role of caretaker and teacher. She taught us English with British words and accents. The first lesson I remember was learning the words for our fingers. We would recite after her, finger, finger, finger, finger, thumb. Each day there was a learning lesson using household items and interactions as lessons for learning English words.

With our entire family coming into their lives, I'm sure it caused a disturbance to their normal routine. There were lots of adjustments for both families navigating the different cultures between the East and the West, like how women didn't have to eat last or how it was okay to walk with our shoes on inside the house, where we were able to run hot showers, flush the toilet, and the amount of readily available food that could be purchased at a grocery store was amazing! Where the cereal aisle had endless choices, and going outside to play without fear was a new concept. Everything was new and incredible; I wanted to touch and smell everything.

Our sponsor family lived near the beach, and we'd go down to explore its beauty. I'd stand in the sand with my bare feet feeling each grain between my toes. The different types of sea life along the beach provided more wonderment and things to explore. I'd find shells and small crabs underneath rocks; however, the water temperature was much colder, and to my dismay, it was not as warm as the river back in Thailand.

I wanted to see and touch everything, to take it all in, from the paved driveway to the brick house where we stayed. I would run my hands along the outside red bricks of our sponsor's house, feeling every dent and crease. At the back of the house, I could see the view of the ocean as the house sat on top of a hillside. I would roll down the backyard, feeling the grass as I came to the bottom of the hill, grabbing a handful of grass along the way.

Sometimes our sponsor mom, Ivy, would take us to the park to play. The concept of actual playgrounds with swing sets, where children were safe to run around, was something I had never seen before. Sitting on the swing, I would watch my legs dangle while looking at the new color of the ground, I thought of how different it was from the gray dirt of Thailand at the refugee camp. It was a nice difference.

Being the youngest, I took up Western culture faster and was like a fish in water. I couldn't wait to learn everything there was to know. Through board games we learned our numbers, alphabet, and words. *Candy Land* and *Shoots & Ladders* were my favorites. Perhaps the colors or pictures of the happy kids being kids without the worries of war are why I gravitated toward those. Kids simply being kids, not children raising children, even at a young age, I knew Bounmy had lost that, but through the board games we played together, life was simple. At least for the time being.

Perhaps it was my longing for a mother figure -my journey of what a mother's love would go through- that carried me through many seasons of hard lessons I learned with Ivy and her daughters.

Our family was taught the culture of the British world by setting the table, learning polite mannerisms, and holding a knife and fork properly. Teatime was very big while making polite conversation with the typical British dry sense of humor, which we practiced each day, like setting the table with a napkin, fork on the left, knife on the right, salad plate, main plate, and teacup with saucer.

Perhaps it was my longing for a mother figure -my journey of what a mother's love would go through- that carried me through many seasons of hard lessons I learned with Ivy and her daughters.

chapter

4

TAYE SOUP AND SOY BEANS

The everyday routine became a classroom to learn English and the culture. From the kitchen to the bathroom, everything was foreign. Eventually, we got the hang of things.

Once I was ready to be enrolled in school, I started kindergarten. Being one of the few Asians, I felt all eyes were on me. There were glares and questions, as though I was a new object of curiosity for the children to explore. I didn't have the grace and wisdom that I do now, and all I wanted was to be like them and fit in. Like many children, their curiosity or lack of understanding made them tease and taunt us. It didn't matter that we were Asians with a

British accent. (That was before being Asian with a British accent was cool. Hollywood was late for the game in those days; it was completely uncool for us during that time.) The children and the teachers didn't know where I fit in.

After being taunted for our Asian names, Taye and Lasoy, the kids would nickname my sister and me "Taye Soup and Soy Beans." Insecurities from my name, Lasoy, given by my mother, would have such a major impact on my life because I didn't feel worthy of the name, not to mention it was hard to pronounce.

The Thai meaning of Lasoy is "*Sweet Golden One.*" The whisper from the enemy was that our mother would still be alive if I were not born, and I was a burden to my sister, Bounmy. This lie weighed heavily on my heart, and the last thing I felt was golden and cherished.

When Ivy suggested we change our names to better assimilate so the kids wouldn't tease us, I jumped at the opportunity without thinking of the significance of her advice, and I saw it as a welcome relief. As a first grader, I was too young to think about the future impact. I wish I could say I picked a profound name and that it came from great research and leaders. However, the mind of a first grader is simple. I chose the name after a cartoon character, Rainbow Brite. I had envisioned myself as one of the characters who lived in a magic

As a first grader, I was too young to think about the future impact.

rainbow land and who went around helping people with special powers while sliding on rainbows with a side-kick unicorn. The name, Katie Cupcake, popped in, and that was that. My sister, Taye, had more sense and practicality. She picked her name after the country singer with long black hair.

Even though I knew English, people couldn't understand my cockney British accent, so I was placed in ESL (English as a Second Language). In those days, learning English took place during recess, which wasn't as sad as it may appear. This gave me relief from the children's taunting.

The teachers poured into us, taking time to understand us. We worked with flashcards, games, and pointing at objects while describing what they were in English. Once the teachers realized I knew English but was using a British accent, they taught me proper English pronunciation. I would go home to Ivy and say with amazement, "It's not wootermelen; it's watermelon. It's not toomaautoes, it's tomatoes." I giggle about those days discovering new words and other words that had different meanings, even though pronounced the same. Like "fags" in British did not have the same meaning in America.

Once the kids discovered my dialect, they would treat me like a new toy, an object of wonderment, and ask me to say words on command so they could be amazed or laugh at me. After a couple of months, I retreated inward and didn't talk; I muted my voice so I wouldn't be seen.

While school was tough, I preferred being teased by the children to being back at the house with our father, who still lived with us at our sponsor family's house. Like I said, he had demons of his own, perhaps it was PTSD from serving in the military. Sometimes I would make excuses for him why I deserved to be struck by him. The accuser, Satan, made me think our father was right, that I was to blame for our mother's death, and I would use this lie to justify why his abuse toward me was okay. I don't recall any moments with him where I felt safe or wanted. I would hide in the backyard, looking up in the clouds, pretending I was anywhere except in the house with him.

Little did I know things would get worse. At the age of seven, in the backyard, our father found me. I discovered an acorn, and he wanted to see what I had in my hand. Reluctantly, I showed him. I don't remember completely how it happened, but he forced me to cut the nut open with a machete. With the acorn in my left hand, holding it between my index finger and thumb, he had me crack it open with the machete. I missed the nut and cut my finger to the bone. With tears streaming from my eyes, I did not cry out loud for fear of further retaliation, so I kept my pain silent without making a sound. Part of me didn't want him to have that satisfaction, and thankfully I didn't cut my finger in half.

When Ivy found me, crying by myself with a bloody index finger, she went to my father and, with both arms together making it in a symbol of an X, she told him what he did was wrong and that he would go to jail. I wish that was the only time Ivy would say those same words to our dad. But there would be more of those X moments, explaining to him in English of jail time. He would play it off like he didn't understand her, but he did.

He may have hurt me, but the machete didn't break my bone. The scar remains as a reminder of that horrible day. The painful memory would live inside, and I carried it as shame, because my father, who was supposed to protect me, left me with yet another scar.

chapter

5

HIDE AND SEEK

At the time of that incident, Bounmy was in her teens. As is typical in Thai culture, our father arranged (accepted money) for her to be with a much older man. She agreed to live with him, even though she didn't want to be away from us. She felt this was the better option and her duty so that she could prepare a way for us to live together in peace, away from our father.

Eventually, Ivy found a small house for our family, roughly 15 miles from Bounmy. Our father found a job working at a manufacturing company. I remember crying to Ivy, pleading for her to let me stay. I didn't want to live with my father, away from my sister, without protection.

Our father's new wife and daughter lived with us. Our stepmom was jealous of us and her bitterness would anger our father who would punish us. She was also under his control, and her younger daughter, Noi, was still a baby and unaware of what was going on. I stayed outside most of the time, away from the chaos and beatings in the house.

On bad days, we would run away to Bounmy, finding any means to get to her, like taking the bus, biking, or walking. Some days we would walk 15 miles in the rain to be in her company for protection. It didn't matter the conditions outside, because the conditions inside were far worse.

One of the brightest moments in those dark days was when I met my first friend. Sarah. She was blonde-haired and blue-eyed, and we bonded right away. She was wild, full of life, and had a family that adored her. They seemed perfect. We rode our bikes to discover every corner of the neighborhood and woods. Endless hours were spent in the creek, building small fires in the woods, and our laughter could be heard across the neighborhood. We wouldn't come home until dark, playing and watching the night sky.

Through her, I grew to understand what it was like to live in America with families who threw birthday parties where I discovered what goody bags were. The concept of receiving goody bags blew my mind, and it was completely different from our culture. In our culture, guests did not receive presents. Opening that small goody bag was like finding pieces of gold. I remember riding on the back of Sarah's bike, her blonde hair glistening in the light, laughing as we rode through the neighborhood. I felt so much happiness that I had found a friend to share laughter with when laughter was little to be had at home.

Sarah accepted me for who I was. We were different in many ways, but also similar in many ways. Though I thought her family was perfect, I later learned they had their own secrets. They were just better at hiding their dysfunction. Maybe that's why we were so close because neither of us wanted to go home. I cherish those days playing outside until sunset; we would know where we were by seeing familiar bikes in the front yards. Sadly, those happy times with Sarah ended abruptly.

One of the games I wasn't good at playing was hide and seek. I played this game many times when our father was drunk and in a tirade. He would find me hiding under the bed and hit me. He would find me hiding under the rug and hit me. He would find me wherever and hit me. When I was caught by him, there would be new bruises on my body the next day. Finding new bruises became part of my life.

Without the protection of Bounmy, our father's anger showed in every form. Though he never touched me sexually, he beat me with whatever was within his reach, including a stick, fishing pole, spoon, hammer, etc. Everything was fair game.

This part of the story is something I wish I could leave out like it never happened. It was the moment I didn't understand why God had given me such a father; I felt like a discarded toy that our father had crushed with his foot into many pieces. It would be one of my darkest days with deep sorrow. It was worse than getting thrown against the wall by my father and left for dead.

Once again, playing hide and seek, I hid in the worst place. It was in an open closet with no doors. Being poor, we had little in the closet to shelter me from our father's sight. With my eyes closed and a frail, bruised body hidden in an open closet, I could hear our father's steps and voice calling out for me. That day, I felt something different. A different type of fear, not the same fear I felt before; this was something different; something bigger. When my eyes closed, I prayed to God or to whoever was out there. I said this phrase over and over in my head, "Please make me invisible. Please make me invisible. Please make me invisible." My entire body was shaking, and I could feel my legs start to buckle out of fear, as my father got closer. He put his hands on my shoulder, but he didn't see me or feel me. I was hidden; made invisible by God. Without a doubt, our mother and God must have known I would not survive the beating that day, and I was hidden and protected by them.

Unfortunately, my other siblings were not so lucky. Our father found them, and I don't think I would have recovered from the beating they took in my place. We were not allowed to return to school for a few days, and when we returned, our teachers called CPS.

Back then, there was no concept of "safe space." We were called into the principal's office where we found Ivy waiting with a police officer and CPS workers. They led us into the cafeteria where the teacher gave us a small tray of breakfast with an apple and a small carton of chocolate milk. They asked me questions about the bruises and about the time our father pulled out the gun and shot at us when our sponsor sister, Cheryl, picked us up. Sadly, there were many of those types of stories.

My shy little voice cracked speaking of the events. Oddly, I felt no shame when recalling these things because they were matter-of-fact regarding what our father had done to me. When the conversation turned to the bruises on my body, shame and rejection set in as I recalled and pointed out the bruises. Like I said, there were no safe places; everything was done out in the open. As I looked around the cafeteria, I could feel and see the other children looking at me like I was some type of freak. I simply wanted it all to stop. I wanted to hide and perhaps be invisible again when I saw their gaze on me. After this incident of recalling the bruises on my body, I would come to refer to our dad as "The Old Man." I would address him simply as the old man.

It took a while for us to be processed in the court system. Meanwhile, we were taken back to Ivy's house.

There, I looked up to her as a mother figure, chasing after what had left me. We formed somewhat of a mother-daughter-figure relationship, which I needed as an eight-year-old girl.

Once the court made its decision, we were asked who we wanted to live with. We all answered, "Bounmy." At this point, Bounmy had moved to Ft. Worth, Texas, to be with a man named Kaydoom, the man my father arranged for her to be with. He was 37 and she was 19 with full custody of us. (Today, our youngest daughter is 19. I cry thinking of her having to raise three children by herself. That hurts my heart, and I cannot imagine her bearing that burden alone without any family to help.)

chapter

6

DUCKLINGS

In America, Bounmy carried the burden of keeping the promise she made to our dying mother of not separating us. She worked tirelessly juggling two jobs, each paying less than $5 an hour. Ylene chose to stay in Washington to live with Ivy, while Vec, Christy, and I chose to be with Bounmy.

We lived in an Asian community in Ft. Worth, Texas. Because we were over the living capacity of the one-bedroom apartment, Bounmy hid us from the manager. We had to make do until she could afford a bigger place. In the Asian community, I met other Asians, yet somehow, I felt different. Because I was influenced heavily by Western and British culture and I had somewhat of a British accent, we didn't fit in, and the community made sure we knew it.

It was a tight-knit and judgmental community, remnants of the old-school Asian community.

Bounmy didn't let that affect her; she was strong and had been through tougher situations, so the old Asian ladies didn't intimidate her. Whatever they dished out, she gave it right back. She made sure we didn't let them get to us and make us feel less than. Since we didn't have parents and followed Bounmy's every step as she took us to and from school, they nicknamed us "Ducklings."

These were some of the best and worst times of my life. Though we didn't have much money, we never lacked love from Bounmy. She took us camping and fishing and did what she could to fill the role of both mother and father. We had household responsibilities; mine was to fill the water bucket in the refrigerator and soak the rice. Christy did laundry, and Vec took care of the trash and heavy lifting.

While Bounmy worked long hours, the three of us were like peas in a pod; we looked out for each other. Christy would take a different direction; she was more of a fighter. Her emotions and rebelliousness would at times get the best of her. I took the approach of not wanting to be seen and didn't want to be more of a burden to Bounmy, so the less stress I could cause, the better off I would be.

I filled my time with schoolwork, collecting stamps and butterflies, and using my imagination to create a better place by writing in my journals. My escape from the Asian community was to daydream, spending endless hours pouring into those journals, filled with drawings and scribbles. They weren't thought-provoking. It was simple messages, notes, and stories a typical elementary child would write.

As much as I wanted to be invisible, I was still seen by bullies in our community, and I was their prime target. One day as I was walking and daydreaming, some kids started taunting me. In the distance, Christy overheard them and came running to protect me, but by the time she got to me, it was too late. One of the boys was throwing stones and rocks at me, and one caught my upper forehead above my right eyebrow.

Afraid that Bounmy would be upset at Christy for not protecting me, we snuck into the apartment, cleaned up my battered forehead with a band-aid, and covered it with a bandana. Luckily, this was during the '80s and the forehead bandanas were in style, so we were able to get by without Bounmy noticing.

As much as I wanted to be invisible, I was still seen by bullies in our community, and I was their prime target.

As much as she tried to provide for us, the struggle of raising three children without help from surviving family members in America was difficult. There was no aunt, uncle, father, mother, or grandparents to lean on for support. Even our Asian community rejected us because they thought we were like a plague. They didn't want their children to play with us. I remember Bounmy shouting back that we didn't want to play with them either and had better things to do.

While she provided for us, Kaydoom kept her in the dark. He didn't allow her access to the bank account. She would give him her entire paycheck and when she asked for money to pay for necessities, he would either tell her no or reluctantly agree and then fights typically ensued. Our financial budget was tight, requiring us to find ways to save on clothing, food, and other expenses, including haircuts. To cut costs, Bounmy decided to take matters into her own hands and cut our hair herself. One day, while she was trimming my hair at home, something caught my eye. I turned my head for just a split second, and at that moment, the scissors accidentally snipped my right ear.

Although we faced financial struggles, we were never short of love from Bounmy. She did her utmost to provide for us and remained with Kaydoom because there were no other viable options, much like our mother had stayed with our father. Bounmy was determined to endure the challenges, driven by a desire not to let our mother down.

Kaydoom would get letters in the mail from Thailand, and he wouldn't let Bounmy read them. He kept her in the dark by not allowing her to read or write in Thai. Eventually, she found the courage to take one of the letters to a Thai co-worker to translate. This is when she discovered he was keeping her money and sending it to his family in Thailand in preparation for them to come to the United States.

After discovering this, Bounmy's heart sank in bewilderment. While she was working to provide for us, he was sending the money to his other family. Bounmy was at a crossroads in her life. With no options and no help, mostly the fear of having to break our mother's promise to keep us together as a family, where was she to go without family and support?

After some time to process and understand the reality of what needed to be done, one day she dropped us off at the community pool to gather her thoughts and go to work. Having grown up with Bounmy, I was overly sensitive to her feelings, and I internalized the fights she and Kaydoom would have and how he would make her feel. She didn't know I noticed; I kept it inside, silently watching but never able to speak up or talk about it. I didn't want to add additional stress to her hardship. When conversations about our time in Laos and Thailand would come up, it was so traumatic that it overfilled her with sadness. It was too much to talk about without tears and triggering painful memories. So, I thought if I kept quiet and went unnoticed, things would be okay, and Bounmy would not be sad or cry.

As a third grader sitting at the edge of the pool and not yet knowing how to swim, the enemy's whisper came back to provide a solution for Bounmy's problems. "If you're not another mouth to feed, she would have enough money to keep everyone together." My third-grade mind believed the lie. Slowly, sliding into the pool, holding on to the edge, and walking deep into the end, I let go. I could feel my body sinking to the bottom of the pool, my chest heavy and my lungs getting tight. All I saw was darkness until I felt a light and opened my eyes. There, a hand appeared like a light in the darkness, stretching and pulling me out safely.

All I saw was darkness, until I felt a light and opened my eyes. There, a hand appeared like a light in the darkness, stretching and pulling me out safely.

Once out of the pool, catching my breath, I looked around for my siblings and the person who saved me. He was nowhere to be found. It was there, on that day, I decided no longer would I be called Lasoy. From that moment, I went by Katie, leaving Lasoy at the bottom of the pool. I didn't feel worthy of the name and the weight it carried, "Sweet Golden One." Going by Katie was much safer and easier to pronounce. So Lasoy was left at the bottom of the abyss, alone in the darkness of the pool for nearly 39 years. Not to mention, I carried the shame of what I tried to do and locked that incident deep down. However, that shame did not stay down; it would come up from time to time, whispering to me how unworthy I was.

chapter

7

ELUSIVE MOTHER FIGURE

Bounmy couldn't find help or a way to keep us all together. It was one of the hardest choices she would make, and to this day, it still breaks her heart. Sadly, there was no other choice except to break the promise made to our dying mother. This was a crossroad in her life where she had no support network and nowhere to go. I always wished there was a place for her to go to get both physical and emotional help so she could keep her promise.

This was a crossroad in her life where she had no support network and nowhere to go.

After exhausting every avenue to keep us together, she had no other option except to send our brother, Vec, back to our abusive father, and she sent my sister, Christy, and me back to Ivy. She had no other choice. She knew no one could replace our mother, even though Ivy would be the caretaker for a while until Bounmy could get back on her feet. Bounmy knew Ivy could never take our mother's place. However, my downfall was chasing after a mother figure that would elude me. If only I had that reassurance that Bounmy did, I would not have chased after that elusive mother figure, which is exactly what I did.

After Ivy agreed to take me and Christy for the time being, we parted ways with Bounmy. I clung to her, crying and wondering what I did wrong and why I was being sent off. Was I being rejected again? What did I do wrong? Was I not good enough? Did I not do all the chores the way she wanted? These were the lies that came whispering as we departed and headed back to the State of Washington.

Staring out the window on the drive to Ivy's house, I thought about how I was going to be good, do the right things, and not be rejected again. Little did I know that in the name of acceptance, I would allow others to make me feel less than.

Living with Ivy and her family came with both wonderful and hurtful memories. Sometimes the hurt was intentional, sometimes not. I felt I truly didn't belong, and I was the object of their pity. A charity case they took in but didn't necessarily accept. I was just an obligation.

It was a balancing act of where I fit in within their family unit. I wasn't adopted nor was I orphaned. Bounmy still wanted me. I was simply on loan for the time being.

So, what exactly is the role of someone on loan? How did I fit in? Was I going to be accepted? How/what could I do to be accepted? These were questions I asked myself. Later, I would discover the answer to the question, "Can good people be hurtful and cruel?" The answer was yes. I lived with the sponsor family from middle school to my junior year in high school, which were the most formative years of my life. Much like many teenagers with hormones, I had questions about life and dealt with insecurities; mine seemed to be amplified.

Christy, on the other hand, went through a rebellious streak where she dressed in goth, stayed out late, and was a handful for Ivy to try to manage. We would fight and make up like most sisters, however, we would protect each other and be there for each other when things were bad. At school, we were so different that people didn't realize we were related. Christy tended to let her anger get the best of her, and she was known as someone not to mess with. On the other hand, I focused on academics, arts, and joining different sports and clubs like Junior Achievement; anything to occupy my time away from home. I excelled in gymnastics. Middle and high school were brutal during the '80s and '90s. There were no anti-bullying programs, kids settled their differences and arguments on the field and in playgrounds, which taught us to either be tough or be a follower.

Christy would own the playground. No one attempted to go near her or get on her bad side. She had a crazy, insane strength (much like our father's) and would find the biggest kid and make sure to swing the first punch. I wanted nothing of the two worlds of being a bully or a follower. I just wanted to go to class and be left alone. However, that would not be the case.

Some teenagers at school would be cruel with their words and actions. Whether it was intentional or not, they were just horrible. They would say and do mean things without thinking, like reminding me that I didn't have a mother and that I wouldn't know how to be one if I ever had children. (Even now, after being out of high school all these years, those words still sting and create insecurities.)

One day, while in the locker room getting ready for the gym class, a group of girls sprayed hair spray all over my body while laughing at me. It was humiliating. One of Christy's friends saw what happened and word got back to her. The two girls later apologized, saying they didn't realize Christy was my sister. Our sisterly fights and struggles went away for a bit, perhaps because we bonded over that incident. The only time I thought of her as being a bully came in handy.

Eventually, Christy's wild streak became too much for Ivy to handle. When Ivy went overseas to London for a long time, Christy would sneak out of the house. She got into tarot cards and wouldn't come home for days. Ivy felt it was time for Christy to go back and live with Bounmy, who had found a small apartment and lived on her own.

So, Christy went back to Texas and left me alone with Ivy, which would have to do for a while. When Bounmy would call to check on me, the conversations were monitored by Ivy, making sure we only spoke in English so that she could understand what was said.

As the days and months went by, phone calls from Bounmy became less frequent. Years later, I learned that she did call but was told I wasn't home. Perhaps as a teenager I wasn't around, but I wasn't told that Bounmy had called. The times we did speak, she would talk about the difficulty and frustrations of raising a rebellious teenager. When she asked how things were going with me, I would tell her things were good, even when they were not. I didn't want her to worry about me.

Once Christy left Ivy's, I was alone. My Thai culture had given way to the American and British ways of living. Hard conversations were swept under the rug, and setting the table properly and having polite conversations was standard. With no one around speaking my native language, I lost it.

Mean Girls

School became harder and lonelier. I found myself in school group limbo, where I wasn't popular, but I also wasn't a nerd. I was just another face at school going from one class to another. Sarah and I would see each other from time to time, but her parents later divorced, and she moved many times to different places, so maintaining our friendship got harder until we eventually stopped communicating.

Without Christy around to keep bullies at bay, the mean girls came from every corner with stupid pranks or harsh words and actions. High school became a wasteland of unsupervised hormones and teenage stupidity. One girl, Kim, had it out for me. She was a big, tall girl with wild, beautiful black hair, and was known to be in and out of the principal's office. She wouldn't address me by my first name; she would either make up a name or call me only by my last name.

One day as we boarded the school bus, I sat next to my childhood girlfriend, Tracy. She had a twin brother that I desperately wanted to impress. I'm sure every girl in school also had a crush on him. While seated next to Tracy, Kim stood next to me and said, "I am going to kick your ass!"

I don't remember what came over me, perhaps I was tired of being picked on. I had a decision to make that day. I was either going to get my ass kicked and be a follower, or I was going to rise up and fight. Within an instant, my body went into auto-fight mode. I immediately kicked her down on the floor with me on top of her. I laid her out with all my frustration from being called names, not fitting in, left behind, and you name it. It was pure rage.

Once the bus driver broke us off, mostly broke me

off of her, I came to my senses, not realizing the damage I had inflicted on her. The only thing I remember was Tracy's brother, the crush, saying, "Wow!" And from that day forward, my friends wouldn't let me forget the day I fought "Big Kim" and won. I didn't take pride in that, and it was the last fistfight I would find myself getting into. Mostly it was because the rage I had inside and took out on "Big Kim" scared me. It didn't make me feel good, but a decision had to be made that day. The details of the fight I told Ivy were different. I said "Big Kim" won because I didn't want to be seen as being improper or a bully. Mostly, I was afraid I'd be shipped away like Christy.

Ironically, "Big Kim" and I had detention together, made up, and became friends. We even made an '80s New Kids on the Block dance move together.

Throughout my high school years, I was a typical teenager. I had moments of not making wise choices, like sneaking out at night to see friends at the beach, dyeing my hair with Sun-In, and lying on the beach until I turned golden brown. But I always remember Bounmy telling us our mother desired for us to have a good education, to make the most of what is given. My focus on schoolwork never left the forefront of my thoughts. I desired to get out of my situation through higher education.

Around my thirteenth birthday, Ivy and Lathe presented me with a gift. Our oldest dog had passed away, so they got me a dog from the pound. It was a half-lab and German shepherd mix. Standing in the doorway, I could see a big, beautiful dog on a leash as Lathe held him. As he brought the dog closer to me, I could tell how strong he was, as he was dragging Lathe closer to me. Standing with a big smile on my face and my hand outstretched, palm facing up so he could smell me, the dog lunged at me, pushing me down on the ground while biting my hand.

> Standing with a big smile on my face and my hand outstretched, palm facing up so he could smell me, the dog lunged at me, pushing me down on the ground while biting my hand. Then he went after my face and neck.

Then he went after my face and neck. I'm not sure how I managed to get him off me but somehow, I was able to get out from under him and get on top of the car.

Lathe finally restrained the dog, and I slowly came down from the top of the car, crying. The dog had torn my face and lips off and clawed my neck and chest. Sitting on Ivy's lap as we headed to the hospital, I pushed past the pain to hold my face together, trying to keep it from falling off. I was covered in blood. The pain was unbearable. All I could do was cry while thinking this was not the 13th birthday party I had envisioned.

I spent nearly two weeks in the hospital for reconstructive surgery with my lips sewn together and bandages over my neck and body. The food would be blended to mush, and I would eat through a straw or tube. I would be another miracle with another scar. Recovery was a slow process.

The dog had to be put down. I felt sorry for him after discovering he was trained to be an attack dog who lived outside, with little to no love. We also learned the owners had given the dog to the pound with instructions not to give it to families with children. That poor dog didn't know any better and he did what he was brought up to do. I think about that dog from time to time, wondering what his life would be like if he had been given love. (Later, Ivy won the civil suit against the pound.)

After the dog attack incident, my relationship with Ivy deepened, and I began to see her as a genuine mother figure. Our bond was characterized by unspoken boundaries regarding what could and couldn't be discussed. Ivy consistently demonstrated kindness and thoughtfulness; qualities I admired greatly. However, our conversations often felt limited to the dynamics of a caregiver and the person she had taken in, leaving me uncertain about where I truly fit into her life.

While living with the British sponsor family brought its share of challenges, particularly in my quest for a maternal connection, it also brought me some of my happiest memories. I cherished the moments Ivy and I spent together attending various plays and engaging in theater activities. She taught me how to prepare one of my favorite dishes, Shepherd's Pie. Our summers were filled with beach vacations, and her laughter, tinged with dry British humor, was infectious. Despite her shortcomings and the fact that she wasn't the mother I had hoped for, I loved her. She became the closest thing I knew to a mother, alongside Bounmy.

During my high school years, Ivy began traveling to London more frequently for work, which often left me alone at home. Her absence took a toll on our relationship, and because of the distance, her marriage also began to unravel. While she was in England, Ivy and Lathe made the difficult decision to divorce. She didn't come home or call to discuss what was going to happen in my situation. It was the typical British way. No one talked about heavy subjects and things were swept under the rug.

Without any real conversation, I heard from Jezel, their adopted daughter, that things were changing at the house, and I needed to go back to live with Bounmy. My plane ticket was purchased within a week, and I needed to pack two bags. One bag had clothing, and the other bag was filled with drawings and a journal book. The rest of my items were stored in the attic, awaiting my return.

chapter

8

ERASED IN THE ATTIC

By this time, Bounmy had moved to North Carolina and was living with a man named Ted, who had a drinking problem. After years of being away, I wasn't sure what it would be like to see her after so many years apart. But when she arrived at the airport, she hadn't changed much. Her beauty and youth remained, along with her toughness.

Arriving in a Southern state was different from the north; from the landscape to how people spoke their words were all new. Adjustments to a new way of life would have to be made. Once again, I was one of the few Asians and, ironically, I expected racism in the south to be like I had experienced in the Pacific Northwest. I was fearful and waiting for people to call me "chink," or tell me to "go back to your home country," and other hateful things. I thought I would have to lie about my race and say I was Hawaiian like I did in high school when I dated a guy whose parents didn't accept Asians.

I'm not saying racism didn't happen in the south, but I am saying that reliving racism in the south did not happen to me. Without many friends at a new school, my senior year allowed me to focus on improving my grades and getting college scholarships. My art teacher became a shining light. She saw my gift and potential and took the time to get to know me and understand my situation. We talked for long hours before and after school and she would give me words of encouragement and advice I desperately needed. She later wrote reference letters to the colleges I applied to.

With a new life in North Carolina, Bounmy still struggled to provide for us. The living conditions were a little better, but she was still with a man who didn't value or respect her. He and I certainly didn't get along. I'd spend hours in my room studying, filling out college applications, and trying to navigate the process of attending college by myself. Then I realized that the cost of college was something we couldn't afford. If we couldn't afford the application cost, how would we pay for college tuition, housing, books, etc.?

Since I graduated with honors and received straight A's, I received letters from top colleges like Duke and Wake Forest, only to hide them and not tell Bounmy. After all, we were struggling to keep the lights on so it would be impossible for her to pay for the school fees and tuition. I didn't want to burden her with my acceptance letters. That would mean she needed a second job to help pay. I wasn't going to ask her to work long hours again, and as much as I desperately wanted to attend college, I threw the college acceptance letters away.

Shortly after graduation, I received a call from Ivy asking if I wanted to come back to Washington State. I sat on this question while rationally thinking through my options. While I didn't want to go back to a family who made me feel like a charity case, I also didn't want to be a further burden to Bounmy, and I wanted to go to college. My conclusion was that life would be easier for Bounmy if she didn't have another mouth to feed, and my chances of going to college would be better with Ivy.

So, I went to Washington State, grateful that Ivy invited me back. But Ivy and I never had a conversation about why I was sent to live with Bounmy or about her divorce. It was the mother-daughter conversation I hoped to have before my return that just never happened. And it was another added feeling that I didn't truly belong with them. I was merely a charity case. Either way, pity or not, it was a way to potentially have a better life and go to college. So, I took it.

Arriving back at Ivy's home was different. After finding a job as a front desk clerk at a hotel, I was free to be on my own. I worked the night shift and saved enough money to enroll at a local community college.

I reconnected with my friend Tracy and her twin brother. We still laugh at the time I fought "Big Kim" and won. Later in life, we discovered each of us had struggles of our own, but during those college years, we carpooled to school together in my worn-out Chevy Cavalier, nicknamed "Old Betsie." We shared fun memories and enjoyed the college years, never allowing alcohol or drugs to become part of our lives, even though it was ramped up during the grunge scene in Seattle.

Those were some of the happiest times and I have cherished them. Unlike most students, I didn't have parents who helped me pay for school. I worked the night shift, full-time at the hotel, and did my homework when all the guests were asleep. I worked from 3 p.m. to midnight, studied, and then went to class at 7 a.m. Working so I could pay for and attend college was difficult, but it was like my mother said, "Make the most of what life gives you."

While at school, another semester came with higher costs for textbooks. I was between paychecks and couldn't afford the $75 for college coursebooks. I saw Ivy pour kindness into others, handing out cash for those who begged on the streets, taking random people into the house, some with less-than-perfect character traits. I decided to ask Ivy if she would loan me the money. When she said no, I was confused but not hurt. I figured she had something else going on, so I didn't take it personally. Deep in my thoughts, I leaned into what Bounmy and our mother taught me about being resourceful. I went into the attic where I had left my few belongings before leaving for North Carolina. Surely, I thought, I had something stored away that could be sold to pay for the book, not that I had anything truly valuable.

The attic wasn't big, and it didn't take long to realize my sponsor family had gotten rid of all my possessions while I was gone. All my pictures, annuals, stamp collections, prom dresses, and awards were gone. Those items didn't matter as much as my beloved journals, drawings, and stories I had written that helped me escape the hardships ... those were all gone. Like it was trash they had simply thrown out without letting me know.

I realized and felt I wasn't even worthy of seventy five dollars.

At that point, I realized I wasn't even worthy of seventy-five dollars. Nothing survived my childhood to show I ever existed. If I died, no one would have cared, and I wouldn't have even made a mark in the world. I was merely trash that was thrown out. I sat there crying, tears streaming down my face, with no one to talk to. I couldn't call Bounmy, nor did I have relatives to talk to. I was alone in the attic; lost, broken, and made to feel like I never existed ... like I was nothing, a nobody.

Out of frustration, sadness, and anger, I cried out to God, or to whoever was out there, asking Him why. He had taken my whole family, given me a father who left me with scars and now, to tell me I didn't exist. Not a single thing that I had survived. I was "a nobody." Why would God inflict this much pain on a nobody? I had nothing, so why take what little I had? What was the point of this life I was dealt?

I was sobbing, tears coming down my cheeks, my heart pounding. Breathing hurt like a sharp pain, cutting and reopening my wounds. It became harder and harder to breathe, and I cried to God that I wanted nothing to do with Him. I didn't want to be involved in anything having to do with heaven and hell or the battle between good and evil. I wanted to live out the life I was dealt, to hide, and to continue being a nobody.

I fell asleep in the attic. When I woke up, my tears were dried on my face. I decided to bury that feeling of worthlessness inside and protect myself. I would never relive that pain if I could help it. I was done. Beaten and defeated. But I was going to live the life I was dealt. What other choice did I have?

chapter

9

IN THE NAME OF ACCEPTANCE

fter pulling myself together, it was time for dinner, and keeping a proper image mattered most to the sponsor family. Bringing up anything painful in front of Ivy would be glossed over and I desperately wanted to be accepted by them. So, I pretended my possessions were still in the attic and life was good. My insecurities held me hostage to take this kind of treatment from them in the name of acceptance. I don't know how I buried these emotions sitting at the dinner table with them. My older self would have given them the finger and made my exit, leaving nothing except smoke trails coming from my car. However, my younger self still had a long way to go in discovering boundaries. So, I sat at the dinner table, politely eating my food, knowing all my belongings were gone as if I never existed.

The next day I went back to work and pretended everything was okay. But it wasn't. I still wondered how I would pay for my textbooks to remain in school. The thought of possibly dropping out of school was looming in my mind, and I had no time to worry about what happened to all my belongings. There were other pressing matters. As my shift was ending, I was handed a small white envelope. Someone had tipped me one hundred dollars for working a busy shift when the snow started falling and flights were canceled. That day, I was the only one able to come to work. I managed to get everyone checked in without help and did the job I was hired to do. But someone noticed my hard work and thought I deserved a tip.

Little did they know how much it meant to me. I held the envelope in disbelief and thought, "I don't understand what this is." It came when I needed it the most. That day, I planned to call the admissions office and drop out of classes. As much as I needed the tip, I knew it would not stretch far enough because the cost of college was too much. Even after taking odd jobs and projects, as well as working at the hotel, I wasn't sure how long I could afford to stay.

During that time, I met with other students to create computer animation skits and short stories. One of my friends mentioned that I would be a good fit at a company called Microsoft; they were starting a project that I might be good at. I looked at him in disbelief. No way would I get hired without a college degree. I didn't think my chances were high, but I went through a couple of rounds of interviews, and by the end, they offered me the position. Not wanting to give the impression that I was too eager and uncertain of what they saw in me, I paused and said, "I think I'm available." But on the inside, I was jumping for joy with excitement and could barely contain myself.

It was a welcome relief because of the cost of college. Then, I decided to put college on hold to get firsthand experience and training at Microsoft. I would take educational courses they provided for coding, leadership training, MS certifications, etc. I was going to make the most of what was given.

Our project was to create a device that would help professionals with notetaking, scheduling, and calendars, and also have an address book. It was called a PDA (personal digital assistant) phone. My job was to set up data collection sites for handwriting samples around the world. This would help convert print and cursive handwriting to text on the PDAs. Little did I know our small group would grow and evolve into the tablets and smartphones we have today.

At Microsoft, I excelled and was promoted to development manager. These were exciting and uncharted times when I found myself leading people who had not only completed college but were graduates from Yale, Harvard, and MIT; they were the best of the best. I was a minority female in a male-dominated industry with half a college degree leading them.

Interestingly, I didn't see it as a career advancement; I wanted to do my job and avoid climbing the corporate ladder as much as possible. I had many insecurities and, deep down, the accuser told me, "Do not be seen and remain quiet." I wouldn't fight for certain projects or against co-workers who took undeserved credit.

One of the things I spearheaded, after realizing our accuracy rate for our training and recognition computer engines was low, was what we call "AI." We would have volunteers come during office hours from 9 a.m. to 5 p.m. to donate handwriting samples at the Redmond, Washington campus. Getting the samples took about an hour. In return for their efforts, they would receive a free Microsoft product. Not a bad deal. While we got volunteers to come, we mostly had older generations from retirement homes. We lacked handwriting samples from younger demographics, our end users, because they couldn't come to us during the hours of 9-5. Later, I pitched the idea of going to them in both classrooms and businesses.

While my team supported the idea, getting it through upper management was difficult. At first, they frowned at the idea based on resources, cost, and time, they didn't think it was a good idea. Finally, I suggested I would take on the responsibility, even if it meant hauling equipment and taking it to the schools and businesses myself. And that's what I did. I lugged every heavy machine, drove across town, and formed relationships with schools, hospitals, and offices, convincing them to give me time and handwriting samples.

Those long hours were hard. I juggled between being out of the office to get the samples and being in the office to attend status meetings, one-on-one meetings, reviews, etc. It was stressful and exhausting. As the months went by, however, it paid off for the project. Even though it was my original idea, I was happy our group benefited, even though at times, I felt my efforts were overlooked and undeserving credit went to others who had superior educational pedigree on paper but lacked common sense or the skillset in real life to get tasks accomplished.

I decided not to let my insecurities get the best of me, especially with the elitists who didn't know my name.

It didn't matter. I was appreciative of being part of the project and its success. I decided not to let my insecurities get the best of me, especially with the elitists who didn't know my name. I loved my group and the different projects I was involved in, and I continued to do the job I was hired to do until I was needed and called elsewhere.

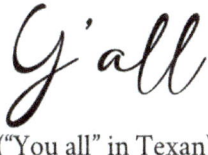

Y'all

("You all" in Texan)

"A new commandment I give unto you, that ye love one another;
as I have loved you, that ye also love one another.
By this shall all men know that ye are my disciples,
if ye have love one to another."
-John 13:34-35

10

THE DATING SCENE

"And it is turned round about by His counsels:
that they may do whatsoever He commandeth
them upon the face of the world in the earth."
~ Job 37:12

As years went by at Microsoft, the company was not immune to the bad hires and opportunists found in most companies. There I learned and grew professionally, forming great friendships. (One became my roommate and a bridesmaid at my wedding.)

While my professional life was thriving, my personal life was lacking. I found myself dating a person who had commitment issues. We spent time discovering restaurants, dancing, and listening to music. He was a welcome distraction from the stressful life at work, even if it was with someone who would be the elusive metrosexual; someone who could never be nailed or define what our relationship was. He was fun, but we would go through seasons of being together and breaking up.

Some of the friends I met at work were graduates from Penn State. During one of my off periods with Mr. Metrosexual, I met a rebound guy, Mike, while watching a Penn State football game with my Microsoft co-worker. I agreed to a date with Mike and, in a moment of weakness, with a cocktail or two involved, one thing led to another. Months went by and my taste buds and body started changing; my breasts were tender. My friend suggested I take a pregnancy test. I must have taken five pregnancy tests and sat in the bathroom at work thinking, crap! This was the worst timing! Having a baby was far from what I wanted or needed.

While my professional life was thriving, my personal life was lacking.

After reality set in, I made a list of the pros and cons of having a baby, where I was in life, and the financial picture of whether I could support a child, healthcare, etc. In my office, I closed my door and stuck a *Post-It* note on the outside that read, "Email only." Work was far from my mind, and the last thing I needed was for my coworkers to see me throwing up with a flushed face.

Staring at my computer screen and the spreadsheet

of pros and cons, I decided to share the news with my boss. Thank goodness she was a female and, at the time, preparing for her maternity leave. I was preparing to take her role while she was on maternity leave. She was the most logical person to go to first.

Inside her office, I could see her stomach nearly eight months and ready to pop. I could feel my breath getting tighter and tighter. Nervous and second-guessing myself, I was about to escape her office when she saw me. Seeing how nervous I was, something out of character for me, she asked if everything was okay. I proceeded to tell her my pregnancy news. She was very "matter of fact" about the news and talked me through the benefits I had at Microsoft. She talked about how having a husband and baby would affect my benefits and life at work being a single mother. I sensed that she was more worried about protecting me from someone who would have access to my finances and stock options. I went home to think through the advice she had given me. While she didn't exactly tell me not to have the baby, the implied hardship of being a single mother at Microsoft would not do me any favors to advance my career. Luckily, Microsoft's benefits were incredible. I had healthcare, dental, vision, stock options, etc. I wouldn't have to pay out of pocket for my entire pregnancy.

Once the decision was made to carry out the pregnancy, I had to navigate through how every choice I made moving forward would affect not only my life but also the life growing inside my womb. Flashback to the time in high school when I was taunted by the mean girls. Their words saying I wouldn't know how to be a mother because I didn't have one, played over and over in my mind. I couldn't sleep at night wondering if I had made the right choice. I may not have a mother, nor would I know how to be one, and perhaps the mean girls were right. Maybe I wouldn't know how to be a mother, but I did know how to be a fighter and protector. And that was what I was going to be: a fighter and protector for my child.

First, I had to tackle my relationship with Mike, the father. There were many things I wanted to give my child, but a divorce was not one of them. After refining the spreadsheet of pros and cons, I came up with my parenting plan. I would tell Mike that we had a good chance of being great friends, but we would not be good partners for marriage. He understood.

Having a Birthing Partner

I also met Susan at the Penn State football-watching parties. She was funny with a dry sense of humor, tough, and didn't take crap from anyone. There was no guessing game about what she thought about certain things. She was brutally honest and caring at the same time. I didn't have to play the games of *Clue* and *Guess Who* about her thoughts and feelings. I liked her at once.

During my pregnancy, Susan and I grew closer. She agreed to be my birthing partner. As the days drew closer to my due date, I had to think of a name for my baby boy. I wanted something strong and beautiful. I thought of the name Kohl, after Germany's leader, Helmut Kohl. He was the chancellor of West Germany and the first politician to walk through the Berlin Wall after it was torn down to unify the end of the Cold War. Kohl is also the brand of the art pencil I used to create artwork that allowed me to escape to faraway places.

I wanted this little person growing inside me to become someone who could create a better place for the world with strength and love. At one of Microsoft's campuses, part of the Berlin Wall was displayed near our dining cafeteria. I walked past it many times and could hear Reagan say, "Mr. Gorbachev, open this gate. Mr. Gorbachev, tear down this wall." The excitement of watching the wall come down and people celebrating live on television never escaped my mind. That celebration reminded me of our time escaping communism in Laos, and the fall of the Berlin Wall gave me hope for what could be.

I wanted this little person growing inside me to become someone who could create a better place for the world with strength and love.

Subconsciously, that was what I wanted for my child; that he would grow up to become a uniter. At night, I would rub my ever-growing stomach while playing soft music and reading to him. I wasn't sure about the person he would become, but at least I wanted him to start his life knowing he felt loved and wanted.

The day came for Kohl's arrival. My bag was prepped, and Susan drove me to the hospital, passing the changing colors of the fall leaves outside my passenger-side window. It was exciting to see something new and change was coming.

Mike, Ivy, and Jezel were meeting us at the hospital. However, I whispered to Susan that I only wanted her and Mike in the room. The moment was overwhelming, and I knew fewer people in the room was what I needed. I was not prepared for more than one person to see my personal parts. The focus had to be on pushing out a life.

With tears streaming out and one more push, Kohl made his appearance. Looking at his face and holding his tiny hands, the happiness and love I felt was more than I could hope for. It was an incredibly beautiful and big milestone.

While I wanted to share that moment with Bounmy, she lived in North Carolina and was making a place for herself. She was doing better after leaving a bad situation and putting herself through culinary school. While working at a country club, she rose to executive chef, overseeing the entire department. While she would have loved to be with me for the birth, her work schedule would not allow it, and I understood. There was so much change going on in my life, the only thing I could handle was being a mother to Kohl.

After being discharged from the hospital, carrying Kohl in my arms, a brief sense of fear arose as we placed him in the car seat. My feeling of being the protector went into overdrive, wondering what would happen on the ride home. Would he be safe? What if we had a wreck? So many *what-ifs* raced through my mind. Then, the fleeting, fearful thoughts left when I saw his face. He was peaceful and asleep, safely tucked away.

We arrived at my place and Mike helped get Kohl out of the car. He handed me the baby carrier, and I carried my son to the front steps of my door by myself. Standing in the doorway, I took a deep breath and opened the door for the first time with another person to take care of. The door opened to an empty room; no flowers, balloons, or family members to help care for us. There would be no greetings from a loved one. It was just Kohl and me. Looking into the lonely, empty room awaiting us, I had to muster every ounce of strength and push back the feeling of inadequacy. This was no time to feel sorry for myself. I had to get myself together and pull up my big girl undies.

On the bright side, I was fortunate to have a career at Microsoft where I could bring Kohl to my office. I set up a Pack 'n Play crib and closed my office door. Most of my meetings were done over the phone or email. But I had my limits, and my career took a setback, which was understandable. Balancing a highly demanding career and a baby was too much to handle. I found myself needing a break and I took it.

chapter

11

U-TURN TO TEXAS

Growing older and being a new mother, I wanted more of a connection to my Asian family. Christy encouraged me to move to Houston and live closer to her. I packed our belongings and did a U-turn to Texas, back to our childhood where Bounmy had raised us.

Before being pregnant with Kohl, while trying to balance work and personal life, online dating was becoming a thing, and I started corresponding with a person I met on Yahoo personals. I kept it private, thinking online dating was for those who couldn't make dating work in real life. This person was from the South, and he was funny, smart, and well-spoken, based on our emails. He was the opposite of who I would typically date; he was a tall Southerner who hunted and fished; not my usual dancing metrosexual type.

At this point, I thought everyone in Texas wore cowboy boots and hats, and the land would be filled with dry cacti. I didn't have boots or a hat, and cacti was not my favorite shrub. Either way, I took a leap of faith to reconnect with my culture. I also thought Texas was the capital of all religions and where Jesus' people resided. The idea of faith, religion, and Jesus was formed by snippets from movies, shows, billboards, music, etc. I had a general idea. I knew I wasn't an atheist, but the Bible wasn't the book choice that would be found among my collections. I was simply a person living my life, not wanting to be seen by either side due to the pain I felt about God.

I knew I wasn't an atheist, but the Bible wasn't the book choice that would be found among my book collections.

When I was in college, even though I didn't want anything to do with religious organizations, I would graciously attend different churches and organizations out of politeness to friends. But there was no deep investment; it was just another place with a roof. The moment the service was over, I would say "Thanks for the invitation" and leave as quickly as I came in, making zero eye contact.

One of the invitations was to attend my first Catholic mass. I said yes because my friend drove, and she was my ride home from a weekend getaway back in my college years. The church was a massive, beautiful cathedral with stained glass windows. Everything was perfectly in place with flowers placed throughout the building. I took in the elaborate architectural designs, which were some of the most beautiful designs I had ever seen. When the service started, the priest would tell people when to stand up and sit down. I looked around the room wondering how the old people's knees were holding up.

Looking at my girlfriend, giving her the glare of "let's go already," something the priest said caught my attention. He talked about the concept of damnation for those who committed suicide. His words took me back to the time I tried to take my own life by letting go of the edge of the pool. The priest's words played in my mind. I had done something horrible that day, and I was walking in damnation and could spend eternity in hell. I wasn't sure if he was right or wrong. But even though it was an attempt to spare Bounmy from disappointing our mother, I felt so much shame and guilt in what I attempted to do. I decided to keep that moment at the pool buried inside so I would not be thought of as a walking damnation and sinner.

Now, I was off to Texas, the heart of where Jesus' people lived.

Off to Texas

Kohl had just turned one when we got settled in Houston. I wanted to pursue other careers, just in case I decided to stay in Texas and make it my home. I enrolled in a program to become a paralegal. If I enjoyed the course, perhaps I would go into law, which was taught at the annex at the University of Houston.

One day I opened my computer and found emails from the Southerner I had corresponded with long ago. I had forgotten about him. My sister, Christy, encouraged me to go out with him, but I preferred to communicate online. After all, what if I were kidnapped? I heard horror stories of people who dated after meeting online. I didn't want to be a statistic. Finally, I agreed to meet him in person at a safe location. The coffee shop at Barnes and Noble was perfect, and I got there early to pick out a public table, just in case.

When I arrived, I could see a tall, big figure coming toward me. The first thing I saw was his belt, which was the same belt as one of my Microsoft co-workers; a geeky computer programmer who had zero social skills and poor hygiene. My initial thought was, "Oh no!" I reached for my jacket, ready to ghost him, but I wasn't quick enough. The 6'4" Southern guy was fast! He said, "Hi, I'm Van. You must be Katie?"

I almost said no, but there was something about him that gave me the presence of both kindness and a protector. I sat back down, and our conversation lasted for hours. Our coffee date turned into dinner at a Chinese restaurant. I'm not sure what made me open up to him about my life or about being a single mother, but I did. Maybe it was the way he made me feel.

After a few dates, mostly me taking him to see Lord of the Rings repeatedly, and him agreeing to go every time, I knew it was time to introduce him to Kohl. He had asked me before about meeting my son, but as a protector, I didn't want formal introductions until I thought things were safe with Van. (I mentioned to Bounmy about meeting Van. She thought I was going to dinner with a Vietnamese girl because Van is a traditional Asian female name. Once she figured out Van was a guy and I wasn't dating a girl, we laughed over the phone.)

God knew Van was the person I needed. Later, I came to discover that he, too, had his personal struggle with the concept of religion and faith. He knew right away he wanted to marry me. I, on the other hand, wasn't sure, but it seemed right for the time being to continue to date him.

Van wanted to spend more time with me and Kohl and would make extra efforts to show that he wanted to include both of us on our dates and outings. On one occasion, he got us tickets to see *Sesame Street Live*. Kohl had just learned to walk and hadn't yet formed full coherent sentences. As we walked by one of the vendors selling balloons, Kohl pointed to the balloons, indicating he wanted one. Van asked if it was okay to get Kohl a balloon. I thought he would come back with a simple balloon but, to my surprise, he came back with a giant floating *Big Bird*. I said, "You didn't have to do that! That balloon is huge, but it's very sweet of you." I could tell it made him happy, and the look in Kohl's eyes was filled with amazement for *Big Bird* until his tiny hand couldn't hold on and, in an instant, *Big Bird* went floating to the ceiling. I thought Van would be upset; however, it was as if nothing had gone wrong. Van, with his natural instincts, picked up Kohl, dried his tears, and said, "It's okay, buddy." He was this gentle giant who simply picked up my son, loved him, and we went out the door singing *Sesame Street* tunes to make Kohl feel better.

When we got into the car, I looked over at Van smiling and, for the first time, I started to fall in love with him. We would later get married and start our life together. Bounmy told me that she had dreams of our mother every day until I married Van. Then our mother stopped coming to her dreams. Maybe it was a sign that things were going to be okay with the life Van and I would build together.

Creating a family came quickly. Before I knew it, I was pregnant with our second son, Patrick John Singleton. His middle name is John, after Van's father. While pregnant with Patrick, I experienced the difference of having a support system. Van poured out his love for me and doted on me. He would gently caress my stomach. I'd lay next to Van at night thinking how safe I felt in his arms and that we had created this beautiful life inside my stomach.

We both wanted Patrick so much and couldn't wait for his arrival.

Van's father was the opposite of my father. Watching their father-and-son interaction made me think of what a healthy father-and-son relationship looked like. In addition, John loved Kohl immediately. It didn't matter that Kohl wasn't his flesh and blood. Kohl was his grandson from the heart, and they were best buds. Endless hours were spent at parks, and he was the grandfather I had hoped to have for our children: loving, kind, and funny. Van's family took both Kohl and me under their wings. Most of all, Van taught me what unconditional love looked like.

The day Patrick was born, as I held his little body in my arms, I knew instantly how much I loved him. When his beautiful little eyes opened for the first time, I gently kissed them, thinking, *may his eyes be like his father's for all the years to come: kind and strong. And may he be a protector for others.* Patrick would later grow up to be just as strong and tall as Van, reaching over 6'4" tall. (It's amazing how a 5'1" woman can push out a giant like that!)

As the years went by with Van and his family, I began to realize the difference in the love they gave me versus my sponsor family. Van's family is open. They don't care about setting the table properly or about how I hold my knife or fork. Their problems are spoken out loud at the table, and that's okay. Van's mother, Debbie, showed me what a mother's love looks like.

The first Christmas I spent with Debbie and John, she gave me a Christmas card with a check inside to buy something for myself. It wasn't about the money. It was about what she wrote inside and the effort to get me a card. She has made me feel accepted and welcomed into their family, with no conditions. I could not have asked for a better mother-in-law. She, too, was the grandmother I hoped for our children. Through Debbie, I now understand what it's like to have a mother's love and support.

Now I understood what Bounmy said about our mother not coming into her dreams anymore. Our mother and God sent me a loving family and our mother no longer needed to appear in Bounmy's dreams to check on me. Of all my insecurities and issues, chasing after a father figure wasn't one of those. It was as though God protected me from that, and brought Van into my life to let me know what unconditional love from a husband looked like.

> It was as though God protected me from that, and brought Van into my life to let me know unconditional love from a husband.

Throughout this time, I tried to keep up my relationship with the sponsor family. After all, I grew up with them during my formative years and, in every sense, they were like family, even though it wasn't official. Ivy would come to visit from time to time. During her visits, I wanted to break through the surface conversations of politeness and go deeper.

The love I felt from Van's family had me wanting to see if I could have the same type of relationship with her. But she would shelve any real conversation by talking about making, serving, or having tea. So, I kept the appearance that things were good. Her last visit to Texas was to see Bounmy. Ivy didn't care for Texas and made it known in our conversations. She didn't like the weather or politics. Even though I had come to call Texas home and had my opinions regarding politics, I would nod my head while sipping tea, not wanting to disappoint her when I did not agree with her opinions about how horrible Texas weather and politics are. Again, I muted my voice in the name of acceptance. The deeper mother-and-daughter relationship I hoped for from Ivy got harder and harder each year.

chapter

12

SEASONS AND REALITIES

Perhaps God knew I wanted a mother/daughter relationship so much that He gave us our third child; a girl. Van knew how much I wanted a girl. When we went to our first ultrasound to find out the sex of the baby, he asked the doctor to triple-check because he did not want to discover my disappointment if he was wrong. The doctor, to our joy, confirmed three times that, yes, we were having a girl to complete our family.

That's when I went on pink overdrive. I shopped for pink dresses; the baby room was painted pink; the baby blanket was pink. I secretly poured out the little girl inside me on the room or things I wanted as a child. It seemed like our daughter's birth came too soon because I enjoyed being pregnant with her, dreaming I would have the mother/daughter relationship I've always wanted.

I wanted her name to symbolize elegance with strength in beauty that regal female leaders, such as Elizabeth the Great, carried. We named her Isabella Irene Singleton, Izzy for short. The day she was born, I looked into the room where I saw everyone I loved. Her brothers and her father. I couldn't ask for more. This precious little girl made us complete. She would make me complete by fulfilling my deepest wish for a daughter. Her little feet and hands were so perfect in my arms. I bent down to kiss her on her tiny forehead thinking,

May she grow up to lead with love and
not be afraid to pursue her dreams.
And if she finds her heart broken, I will be
here to hold her in my loving arms.

With our family complete, our marriage went through many seasons of hard times through the reality of raising three children without family support nearby. We would have to make the most of what was given. I was a fierce protector of our children. I made up my mind long ago that if I ever had children, I would protect them from what I went through with our father. The burden I had inside was not going to reach our children. I would protect them from my past and how I grew up because it was such a sad story, and that crutch would not be placed on them. It was hard enough for me to carry, and I would do everything I could to protect them from those feelings and keep them away from our father. I would not speak to them about the details of coming to America and the scars on my body. They would know general details and nothing more. I had to spare them from the heaviness of how I grew up.

I made up my mind long ago if I ever had children, I would protect them from what I went through with our father.

It wasn't until they were in college that I started opening up to them about the details of my life. I wanted to wait until they were mature enough to handle the tough, hurtful, broken conversations of the Asian side of the family.

Navigating Parenthood

As Van advanced in his career, his job required him to travel more often, leaving me home alone with the three kids. Most times, I raised our children doing the job of a single mother. Not intentionally, but that's what was needed of me. Van would lovingly say, "I make the living; you make life worth living." And that's what we agreed on together through hard times, good times, and the times in between, we were each other's partner.

With Van traveling more frequently, I had to learn to navigate carpools, homework, dinners, and after-school activities by myself, for the most part. I formed and joined different moms' groups to get parenting advice and to have playdates for our children, and I formed many friendships. We leaned on each other to help with pick-up and drop-off duties at school, chaperoning, and play dates. I took every opportunity to be available for our children, making sure they were loved, and I supported them in their school activities and sports. I was immersed as a stay-at-home mom, volunteering as a band mom, booster club, etc. Life was going smoothly, except something was missing and I wanted to connect to my heritage and roots. Most of my friends were Caucasians and not too many people were Thai or Laos.

During the journey of motherhood, I slowly lowered my guard about God. It helped that I lived in Texas, the capital of Jesus' people, which made it difficult to escape conversations about faith, God, Jesus, etc. I jokingly told friends in Seattle that Texas has three big things. Steak houses, furniture stores, and churches. Throw a rock and you'll hit one of them within a two-mile radius.

From time to time, friends would ask me to attend church service, and I would politely decline and walk the other way. My mind always went back to that time in the Catholic church and how the priest made me feel. I knew I couldn't step inside another church building. If I did, I would just tune things out and be polite. The thought of damnation would play over in my head, wondering if what I did was wrong or if I was okay since I survived. Either way, I felt shame and guilt and would not speak about it to anyone. I didn't know how much havoc the guilt of that incident would wreak in my life, especially in my relationship with Van.

Motherhood changed everything. I no longer thought only of myself. In some way, God used our kids to soften my heart, teaching me how to deal with relationships, especially with my father's abuse, and to start my faith journey with Him. God knew Texas was where I needed to be to break my stubbornness. There were no longer coincidences I could ignore; life has a way of maturing us as parents. Learning to forgive is a big part. God was setting me up to give grace to those who perhaps didn't deserve it.

God used our kids to soften my heart, teaching me how to deal with relationships, especially with my father's abuse, and to start my faith journey with Him.

As a child, I had such a disconnect with our father. The last time I saw or spoke to him was the day CPS took me away; the day God put his wings around me in that small closet, making me invisible, protecting me from his abuse. When I was describing my bruises to CPS and the police officer in the school cafeteria, I felt nothing for our dad. Nothing. My relationship with him was that he was a person who hit.

I don't remember a time sitting and having a meal with him, or him taking me anywhere. I had no good memories with him.

However, Bounmy had a different relationship with him. Even though he was also abusive to her, she held to the Asian custom of honoring your parents. Perhaps I was more Westernized, but I held the belief that respect is earned, and he certainly did not earn my respect. She, however, held to the Eastern cultural belief of "respect your parents at all costs." To me, this was an odd way of thinking. I didn't get it, but I accepted it. I had seen how he hit her and tried to sell her, and that's just the surface of all he had done.

Since I had already made peace with my feelings for our father, I supported Bounmy's relationship with him, but I wanted nothing to do with him. I didn't introduce our children to him. I didn't even utter his name, and I referred to him as "the old man." I wanted to protect them from his abuse and toxicity. But I am Bounmy's greatest supporter and would go to the ends of the earth for her, even if it meant supporting her relationship with our father.

So, when our father was nearing the end of his life at the age of 80, Bounmy wanted to bring him to Texas to care for him. I was supportive and willing to help him get his medical care, driver's license, and everything else he needed to relocate to a different state. The last time I saw him, he was in his prime, tall, strong, and with a full head of hair. He was big and strong with a commanding voice. The day Bounmy brought him to my house, he looked much different than the man I once knew. He was in a wheelchair, frail, and had lost much of his hair. His voice was weak. It was not the commanding and forceful voice I remembered. I looked at him and felt sorry for him. In that moment, I forgave our father. Not because he deserved it, but because I loved Bounmy and, to help her, I had to forgive him and release myself from the hurt he had inflicted on me. For the first time, I introduced him to our kids. This would be the first and last time they would meet him.

Shortly after, he decided to go back to Hawaii to live out his last days. A year later, he passed away and Bounmy needed my help to honor his Thai burial. We went to Hawaii. I went to bury the man I knew and Bounmy went to bury her father. During his funeral, my siblings were emotional from his passing. None of them wanted to speak, either because they were too emotional or because they didn't want to speak in public. Bounmy looked at me as we were sitting, with a Kleenex in her hand, eyes swollen with tears, and she asked me if I could get up to speak. I was not sure how to respond, but seeing her crying and unable to find words, reluctantly, I caved. There was no other option.

I stood in front of people I barely knew, a person who could barely speak Thai, and gave the eulogy for a man who had inflicted so many outward scars. I was not prepared to do that, but God knew I needed to do it in order to release myself from my worldly father so I could make a way to know Him as my Heavenly Father. This gave me closure and grace for something I would need to learn for other relationships in my life, especially raising our children and developing friendships.

chapter

13

WHY NOT YOU?

We did not push the idea of religion on our children or make them attend church service. We wanted them to discover their faith, which was not something we discussed at home. It also wasn't something we would deny our children. When they were asked by friends to attend church service or VBS, I'd say yes.

As parents, our best and worst days can be found in our children's tears. When Patrick was going through a tough year, he needed more than what the public school had to offer. Patrick was always the biggest kid at school. He is our gentle giant and was

> As parents, our best and worst of days can be found in our children's tears.

often mistaken for being much older than his actual age. Living in Texas, everything is bigger. If you're over 6 feet and nearly 340 pounds as a freshman, football is automatically assumed as your sport. High school would be a tough season for Patrick's growth, both physically and mentally.

Once we made the decision that he needed something more than what public school could offer, we moved him to a Christian school. There, Patrick grew to become a man, and his faith took flight. Meanwhile, Kohl's faith took an even bigger flight. God was working in our kids to help me grow my faith.

As parents, we automatically assume we will be the ones leading and teaching our kids. In this case, our kids were teaching me about God and His faithfulness. It was a revelation and a way for me to slowly let down my guard. However, God needed to give me a bigger nudge through friendships, and He needed for me to be still. That's when the world did indeed stand still, via a lockdown, and God was on the move.

While I had successfully met a lot of wonderful mom friends in the community, I was still longing to meet other Thai and Lao girlfriends to share my culture. It was something I had always wanted, and I thought it was time to connect closer to my heritage. I thought having deep friendships meant I needed someone who looked like me, spoke the same language, and ate the same food. That would be one of the toughest lessons I'd have to learn.

Friendship isn't rooted in outside appearances; it's the qualities within that matter.

Sometimes, God gives us what we want to teach us a lesson so we can grow. And that's what he did. He gave me a friend who looked like me, spoke like me, and ate the same food. This led to one of my biggest betrayals from a Lao girlfriend named Teki. We instantly connected because we shared similar professional experiences, language, and a love for our culture's food. I would share with her the intimate details of my life. Her friendship meant a lot and helped me connect back to my heritage. I did not know she was opening the wounds I had locked deep inside. Things in our friendship seemed to be going great until they didn't.

Friendship isn't rooted in outside appearances; it's the qualities within that matter.

Without my knowledge and behind my back, Teki mentioned issues from my past with our other Asian friends, twisting and manipulating the things I confidentially shared with her. She brought up things that happened over thirty years ago and somehow managed to turn those things against me. I don't know why she did it. Perhaps she thought she was protecting me. I don't think she meant it with malice, perhaps she was going through things herself, and the enemy used her as a way to get to me by bringing up hurt feelings and reminders of whispers that told me I was not good enough.

She would tell others that Katie was not my real name, as if I was the only one who ever went by my middle name. For some reason, the enemy needed to bring me back to the shame and guilt of being a burden when I left the name Lasoy at the bottom of the pool. They made something innocent to be perverse, and they did not know it was a deep wound I had buried inside. Nothing made sense as to why those closest to me would spew such hatred and outright lies about how I grew up. It was a hard and vulnerable time of my life. I spent weeks crying, unable to get out of bed because of the betrayal of a friendship, but it was what I needed from God to help expose the feelings that were buried and locked deep inside.

While dealing with the loss of Teki's friendship, I was also trying to figure out where I was in my relationship with my sponsor family. Because I had distanced further from them, I still wanted their love and approval. For Christmas, Mother's Day, and birthdays, I would send cards to Ivy and the family, but I received little response from them. Our phone calls drifted.

When I wrote cards or notes to them, I would sit in the dining room and Van would sit in the living room with his back toward me. That frustrated me.

One day Van and I argued about him not helping me write Christmas cards and sitting with his back to me, ignoring me. I wasn't prepared for his reply. "I was not ignoring you. Do you know why I sit with my back facing you, year after year, while you write cards to Ivy and her family? I hate seeing the disappointment in your eyes and how it makes you feel when you do not get Christmas cards or phone calls, especially around Mother's Day and your birthday. Do you not think I could hear you silently cry yourself to sleep at night because of how much you hurt? I was tired of seeing you go through that year after year, and I cannot stand to watch you write cards to people who do not deserve your love. I love you and was willing to let you do what you have to do, but I was not going to watch you write those cards."

Van was right. I needed to accept my place within their family and release myself from them. God would make sure it was okay, even if it meant more hard life lessons.

Lockdown of 2020

Those hard lessons came during the lockdown in 2020. Ironically, it took a pandemic for me to be still so that God could work in me. By this point, I was almost ready. God would have to bring someone bold with a bigger personality and who was on fire for Him.

While the world was trying to figure out the new normal, high school seniors had to adjust and forego their traditional senior activities. Though we didn't have a senior that year, my heart went out to them and their families, so I decided to make some fun "ding-dong-ditch" goody bags for seniors with t-shirts that read, "Senior Skip Day

Champions." I created the bags myself and invited others on the high school Mom's Facebook page to come and help me assemble them.

This tall, dark-headed lady, wearing bright red lipstick and an animal print shirt, was at my front door, on fire for Jesus. She was twice my height and her name was Jennifer. I knew she lived in our neighborhood because I had seen her around town for many years while living in our community. My natural response to any form of religion and Jesus' people was to steer clear, so when I would see her coming toward me, I would politely avoid her or do a U-turn. I just wanted to be left alone, not add or take away from conversations about religion, etc. I simply wanted to be left alone and live out the life I was given, but God had different plans.

God brought a bold, on-fire-for-Jesus, person to help me stuff goody bags for the seniors. At the time, her son was a senior and I could feel her heartbreak about his senior year. As we talked about the lockdown, I grew to know her more. When she asked me about faith or got on the subject of God, I would politely change the subject, but somehow the conversation always went back to faith. It was as though God would not let me off the hook, and I started opening up about my background and feelings toward God to the most unlikely person.

After Jennifer started to break down the wall for me to discuss my relationship with God, I felt something different. Then, on a phone call one day, she asked if I wanted to receive Jesus Christ as my Savior. I said yes, and with tears flowing, I could feel the heaviness break down, along with the wall I had built against God and His people.

Nights became increasingly harder to fall asleep, as though I couldn't turn off my brain about God. He would bring me back to certain parts of my life, showing me where He was and how He protected us. It was as though He was showing me movie reels of my past, present, and future. I started dreaming of things that I could remember. I saw things differently. The small voice I would hear throughout my life got louder and louder.

One day when I was home alone, God spoke to me. Not in a weird way, not in an audible voice, but it was Him. We were having a conversation in my mind and out loud at the same time. I could feel His presence around me. Sobbing, I could feel His gentleness and power at the same time. There was no burning bush, just laundry waiting to be folded, but I could hear Him say, "Stop chasing others. I am your true Father."

I must have cried for hours that day. He would softly tell me to talk to both my sister and Van about my wall and what I had kept inside about being a burden and leaving Lasoy at the bottom of the pool. Mostly, He asked me to help build His kingdom. My body was shaking, my legs felt like Jello, and my chest was about to burst. However, I was defiant and not ready. I just cried and spoke with him, "Please not me. Please let it be somebody else. I am a nobody, nothing." I then went further to open my hurt and rejection of what I had felt from Him.

> "Where were you during all those times when I was left for dead, broken, beaten, and abandoned by those who were supposed to love and protect me? You could have used me during all those broken moments, but instead, I felt rejected and abandoned by you. All for what? To help build a kingdom for those who didn't want me? For those who made fun of my name? For those who betrayed my trust? For those who left me wounded and riddled with scars? For those who said they were my sisters and friends only to use my insecurities against me? There are a million great, Jesus-loving, Bible-thumping, holy roller Christians who would gladly write your book. My family tree has been cut down to only five of us on earth. I have nothing to offer, I am nobody. Why bring up my pain for others to pour salt on? Why reopen those wounds from so long ago? Why expose myself when my life is finally good, where I can do all the things most people could only dream of? Why now and why me?"

God replied, "Why not you?"

chapter

14

PURSUED BY GOD

knew what I had to do, but I was so deeply wounded, it would take me a little longer to be obedient. If others had heard God speak to them, they would immediately agree to fulfill His assignment, but not me. I was still wrestling with the enemy's whisper of lies. I was afraid of abandonment, shame, and being a burden, as though there was an internal battle. It was hard to let go of the things I carried inside for so long. Some days, I would heed God's voice, while on other days, His whispers became too difficult to ignore. In those moments, I would find myself getting into the car and driving alone, hoping to drown out the voice. Yet, no matter how far I drove or how loud I'd play the music to silence His calling, His presence remained with me, unwavering and persistent. I didn't want to be seen by the two sides; neither good nor evil, nor did I think I was the right person when there were so many other great Christians with much more experience of being in the church. I was an outsider, so how could God use me? I didn't own a Bible. I knew little about different religions. I couldn't tell you the differences between a Baptist and a Lutheran, or what exactly a Believer was. The insecurities I carried for so long delayed my obedience, but God was aware of my struggles and wounds. He was intricately involved in the details of my life and was actively working behind the scenes. I just had no idea how profound His plans for my healing would turn out to be.

Since the lockdown had everyone at home with few places opened for in-person activities, a friend mentioned a church that was still having services. We had three kids at home, seven dogs, and a mother-in-law living with us. Going anywhere was a welcome relief, even if it was church. I just needed to get out of the house to breathe.

The church was called Rock Creek Church and was open to welcome the lost, broken, and those who needed to get out. I fit into all three of those categories. As I entered the building, I followed my usual routine of avoiding eye contact with churchgoers. I made a direct dash to locate my friend in the main auditorium. Uncertain about what awaited me, the lights began to dim and worship music started playing. I could feel my body getting warmer, then my eyes started filling with tears from the worship music.

I could hardly breathe and couldn't stop the flow of tears. It was getting harder to breathe inside the auditorium, so I stepped out to catch my breath and went into the bathroom. Walking out of the bathroom, I planned on leaving, but as I made my way toward the exit, I heard music coming from the auditorium, wooing me back inside.

After I returned to my seat, tears flowed harder. I'm not a crier and I didn't want anyone to see me in that state. I wondered, "Can things get worse?" Then my legs felt as though they were going to give way. My friend hugged me and whispered, "That's the Holy Spirit." Tears flowed even more, and no amount of tissue was going to help. Trying to stop the tears was useless, so I just let them flow as I listened to the music.

Once the music stopped, I thought I was safe. Then Pastor Brad walked on stage and talked about sowing seeds, which are God's words. Not only was I crying, but my body was mesmerized and completely still as I hung on to his every word. I had no idea about the Bible passage he was speaking of, nor any passage in the Bible, as I didn't own one. My idea of the Bible was formed by what the world had told me from movies, music, commercials, billboards, etc. I thought the Bible contained stories of perfect saints with halos and, at the beginning of the Bible, I thought there would be a twelve-step program for sinners to repent, and the Virgin Mary was the poster child of what a perfect mother should look like. My life was nothing compared to the cast of characters and their hard journeys that I would soon come to discover.

After Pastor Brad's sermon encouraging believers to be "all in for God," I was finally comfortable with thoughts of opening the Bible. I wanted to learn about God and deal with my inner feelings, so bold Jennifer recommended a counselor named Vicki, trained in the Word of God. I took her suggestion and, with guidance from the counselor, I was able to share and open my hurts and hangups with God.

I spent hours scouring the Christian bookstore looking for my own Bible. I settled on the King James Version and, to say the least, it was confusing. I had a hard time pronouncing the names and cities and discovered there were multiple Mary's and John's, which made more sense. All this time, I had assumed that John might have possessed special powers that allowed him for time travel. Needless to say, I was relieved to find out that teleportation for John didn't actually occur. But the inner voice, the Holy Spirit within me, was telling me to be obedient if I truly wanted to know Him. God wanted me to put in the work, and it would not come easy. So, I put in the work, and purchased books on top of books, from historical settings, timelines, audibles, and maps. Day after day, my Amazon cart was filled with books on Jesus, religion, the Hebrew language, and journals to record what I was learning. I prayed each night asking God to guide me and give me His wisdom to untangle what was taught to me by the world.

Facing My Biggest Fear

During this time, Kohl had become more involved at his church in college and started his faith journey. Patrick was away at college pursuing his own. With multitudes of books I had purchased about God, I was still seeking and praying for something that would help my faith journey. I just didn't know what yet. Until, one day as I was cleaning Patrick's room, I stumbled across a book called, *From Good to Great in God's Eyes*, by Chip Ingram. It was as though I stumbled across gold. This was one of the books other than the Bible that forever changed my life and helped my restoration. I purchased Chip's book in hardcover version, and I also purchased them as audibles. I listened to both the Bible and Chip's book on long road trips because I needed to hear them several times to fully understand the text. I looked up words and places I didn't understand. Meanwhile, God was reminding me to break down the wall with Bounmy and Van, and to share my pain with them about the pool incident and all the sadness I kept inside.

Through the course of our marriage, Van had pestered me about getting my citizenship. Something so easy caused such a strain on our marriage. Since I didn't feel worthy of the name Lasoy, *"Sweet Golden One,"* I felt it didn't matter if I got my citizenship. I was able to fly out of the country through a reentry visa and, after 911, being an American seemed more dangerous. I was content with not sticking out.

Van wanted to travel and take me to different countries. I used excuses about raising our children and how hard it would be to travel with them, but Van was relentless and asked if there was something I wasn't telling him. He was correct. I was afraid if I told Van, he would think less of me. The priest in the Catholic church told me that I was a damnation walking around, and others would think I was trash for trying to take my own life. I felt like I was a horrible person. Van loved me so much; I could not bear the thought of him looking at me differently. I feared he would abandon me.

There were so many times I wanted to tell him why I wouldn't get my citizenship. It would be on the tip of my tongue, but the words wouldn't come out, as though I was held captive by fear. I could take anything life threw at me, but I couldn't take the disappointment in Van's eyes, which would have broken that tiny thread holding me together. My fear kept Van at arm's length, and it kept my wall up until God told me to tell my husband. I had to trust God, so I did.

One day I was in our walk-in closet getting dressed when Van came in and had enough of me avoiding the subject of my citizenship. He said, "Enough is enough. We are traveling this year out of the country, and I want to spend it with my best friend." Inside our closet, yes, the best place to have a heavy conversation, words, and tears came out for the first time. Van was the first person I told about the pool incident, how I felt like a burden and blamed myself for my mother's death, and mostly, how I was afraid of him leaving me. I couldn't bear to see the disappointment in his eyes, and I did not want him to think less of me. I didn't realize how hard I was crying, my body shaking. There in the closet, Van held me as I buried my sobbing face in his chest.

He lifted my chin and said, "That's it," with a smile. Those simple words were all I needed, no lengthy drawn-out conversation. Just "that's it," which was all I needed. It wasn't the horrible scenario the enemy made me believe would happen. Van loved me for being me and the heavy burden and weight instantly left. I loved Van and he loved me. After that, I started the process of becoming a citizen. (Today, I am a proud citizen of the United States of America.)

Van loved me for being me and the heavy burden and weight instantly left.

The next person I had to tell was Bounmy. I wasn't sure how she would take it and, honestly, I think she had been waiting for this conversation. Dialing her number, it seemed like an eternity before she answered. I thought, "Okay, if she doesn't pick up, that means it's not the right time." With a click, Bounmy answered.

We started our typical conversation about food, weather, gardening, etc. I could hear God saying, "Tell her, just tell her. It will be okay." So there, between what I ate for lunch and dinner, I blurted it out. "Do you want to know why I have a wall up? I need to tell you something that happened long ago at the pool in Fort Worth." At once, everything poured out with tears. Bounmy replied, "I've always wanted our conversations to be deeper, and I knew something was holding you back, but I didn't want to press you."

I told her how I felt I was a burden to her, and I was sorry our mother passed away and made her promise to take care of us. She cried and said, "I was her daughter and would not change anything." We spoke for over two hours, revisiting our childhood, how she raised us, and the time I lived with Ivy.

This conversation was different; the walls were down to speak freely about the things we both held inside. God strengthened our relationship. He dissipated the lies from the enemy and reminded us that He, along with our mother, had been watching over and protecting us all these years, guiding our steps as a loving Father does.

Kintsugi

(Joining with gold in Japanese)

"But He knows the way that I take;
When He has tested me, I shall come forth as gold."
-Job 23:10

chapter

15

LASOY COMING UP FOR AIR

"Therefore we are buried with him by baptism
into death: that like as Christ was raised up
from the dead by the glory of the Father, even
so we also should walk in newness of life."
~ Romans 6:4

As months went by, I grew deeper in my walk of faith and in absorbing everything I could about Jesus and the Bible. My journey of finding my place in God's kingdom began to unfold. I continued going to church and attended my first Bible study, from the book of Genesis, about the story of Joseph and his family. This lesson came at the perfect time as I was dealing with my relationship with my sponsor family.

When the son of my sponsor sister, Jezel, was getting married, I did not receive an invitation to his wedding. While my relationship with Ivy left me wanting more, I knew where I stood. However, I could not imagine why they would not invite me to the wedding of my almost-nephew.

Jezel's son came to Texas to play baseball and, though my relationship with Jezel wasn't strong, her son was a great person and I loved him. Jezel would always make me feel that she was Ivy's favorite daughter, and what she said goes. Her son dared to tell me he wanted me to attend his wedding, but his mother didn't think it was a good idea. I told him I would support their wishes. I didn't hold it against him, and I sent them a gift and wished them the best.

After knowing I was intentionally left out, I received a phone call from my sponsor sister, Cheryl, telling me all the wonderful things from the wedding, giving every detail. Once again, in the name of acceptance, even though I knew they left me out of the wedding intentionally, I listened to her for an hour as she went through all the details. It was as though she meant to rub it in my face. I knew I should have spoken up and stood up for myself, but I didn't because of my insecurities. After getting off the phone, I just cried. How could this person, knowing I was deliberately left out, be so hurtful and mean-spirited toward me? Later that night, I wondered, "Why did I do that? Why didn't I just hang up the phone?" I cried and prayed, wondering if perhaps I wasn't meant to be part of special occasions.

God used our children to help answer that question. One day, I received a call from Kohl, telling me he was getting baptized, and he sent the most beautiful pictures. It was as though everything aligned perfectly one after the other. After getting Kohl's photos of his baptism, I received an email from Rock Creek Church letting me know a baptism was going to take place and where to sign up. As I looked up from the email, Patrick walked in and asked me what was going on. I said, "Kohl just got baptized. Would you like to get baptized with me?" He responded, "I would love to." I had so much joy and couldn't believe he agreed to do this with me. He bent down where I was sitting and hugged me saying, "I love you, Mom." I couldn't believe he said yes, thinking *what teenager would agree to get baptized with his mom and do it in such a loving way?*

He, too, had overcome his storm and had seen the transformation from the other side. For Patrick, it was a literal transformation on his weight loss journey. He went from 340 pounds to 265 pounds. I immediately responded yes to the email for both me and Patrick before we changed our minds. I had no idea what to expect or even what a baptism was, but I knew it involved water, and some people wore white and were submerged under water. I was trusting God on this journey.

My baptism at Rock Creek Church was held on September 12, 2021, the day after 9/11, a day of immense turmoil, transformed the following day into a day of great joy for me. Perhaps God was telling me something. As I stood in the hallway waiting for my turn with Pastor Greg, a flood of memories came rushing back. The journey to America, surviving two cultures, being raised by my sister, working at Microsoft, marrying my wonderful husband, and raising our three incredible children. Each experience led me closer to this momentous day where I was surrounded by God's love and grace. All I could see was God, the water, and myself. Tears of sadness were replaced with tears of gratitude, belonging, and unconditional love.

Stepping onto the stage and into the water, I felt an overwhelming wave of nervousness. I wasn't certain what would happen, and I certainly didn't expect to be ugly crying in front of a large audience. As I stood there, it felt as though I was completely alone, disconnected from the audience and the music. Just God, Pastor Greg, and me. (Later I learned Coffey Anderson was on stage singing "Amazing Grace.") When I accepted Jesus into my heart, as I emerged from the water, Lasoy came up for air for the first time, no longer held at the bottom of the pool. It was the day the chains of hopelessness, abandonment, and shame were broken, no longer holding me captive by the lies of the enemy; the day God redeemed me.

Finally, I accepted that I was truly a child of God. I realized that throughout my life, even when I was running from Him, He still pursued me. Even when I didn't want Him, He wanted me. Even though I thought I was a nobody, He still wanted me. Throughout my journey, God never left me; He patiently waited for and pursued me until I was ready to embrace His love. I had to go through the ugliness to see His beauty. I could vividly recall moments when He was working through me saying, "Stop chasing after other people's love; rest and find comfort in Me." It was as though a switch had been flipped, and I instantly knew to whom I belonged.

As I took that first breath out of the water, seeing Pastor Greg grinning from ear to ear, tears of relief filled my eyes. I was overwhelmed with emotions, as the song, "Amazing Grace," so beautifully captures. *My chains are gone; I've been set free.* I was washed and made new. I was reborn, filled with purpose. God had wiped the tears of sadness and replaced them with tears of gratitude. No longer did I feel like a burden; I was reborn and surrounded by the love of God. The day was even more special because I had the privilege of being baptized alongside my middle child.

Seeing Patrick join me in the water, I realized how God had given me everything I have always longed for. He redeemed me as a mother, proving the enemy's lies wrong.

Even though I didn't have a mother to share stories with or teach me about life, God had different plans to teach me about motherhood. He not only blessed me with three amazing children, but He used them as a guiding force in my life that led me to this transformative moment. It was a special time when I was not excluded but I belonged and was wanted. It's as though God answered my question about whether I was meant for special occasions. He exceeded the answer I expected. He redeemed me as a mother and made me realize that I didn't need a special occasion to be wanted by Him.

Isabella watched from the audience as Patrick stood by my side in the water. Kohl had played a significant role in leading me to say yes to baptism. If God had taken me home that day, I would know I had done something right as a mother. Having two godly sons and a daughter who was growing closer to God brought me immeasurable pride and joy as a parent. My heart swelled with love and gratitude, knowing our children had given me the greatest gift – a sense of belonging and the chance to be the mother I always wanted. Through them, I became the mother I longed for all my life. Thank you, God.

No words could capture the depth of my gratitude nor the importance of this experience for someone who had, at one time, felt lost and alone. I could not believe what was happening. Patrick held me as tears of joy streamed down my face. I didn't realize people in the audience were watching me ugly cry until someone handed me a towel.

Patrick hugged me as we got out of the water, telling me that everything would be okay. Indeed, things were going to be okay.

After that day, I chose to celebrate the unique combination of my first and middle name. Lasoy Katie, the *"Sweet Golden One."* From that point on, I carried myself with a little more confidence, as silly as it may sound, and I started to embrace the beauty of both Lasoy and Katie, the East and the West.

chapter

16

WASHED AND REDEEMED

*"But He knows the way that I take; when He
has tested me, I shall come forth as gold."*
~ Job 23:10

A friend once told me that there are two crucial dates in our lives: the day we are born and the day we discover our purpose. The day I came up for air after my baptism was a pivotal moment, a day God brought beauty to my scars. He washed away the lies that kept me drowning in hurt, guilt, and shame. Instantly, as if the light switch had been turned on to the beauty of my name, I changed my Facebook name to Lasoy Katie Singleton. To others, this would probably mean nothing.

But to me, it was the first time I truly felt free and alive. It would take some time for people to get used to saying my Thai name, and I would slowly accept the name given to me by our mother and God.

After discovering more about the stories in the Bible, I learned that all the people were broken and flawed. Some were even murderers, but God would redeem them and use them for His purpose. It helped me to know I was not the only one struggling with my name and identity. The story of Joseph and how he had forgiven his family and persevered, regardless of the horrible situation he was thrown in, helped my healing process.

Once I started going by my name, Lasoy, a friend mentioned that my name reminded her of Kintsugi, an ancient Japanese art form that masterfully transforms broken pottery by mending its fractures with powdered gold. This intricate process involves meticulous cleaning, grooming, treatment, healing, and ultimately, enhancement of the object. Translated as "golden joints," Kintsugi honors the object's past and the experiences it has endured. Rather than concealing its imperfections, this art form embraces the break as an integral part of the piece's story and elevates its value and aesthetics.

I thought of the meaning of my Thai name, Lasoy, *"Sweet Golden One."* Just like those broken jars, I felt shattered into a million pieces from my past, then God, as the ultimate craftsman, took what was broken and mended my scars with gold to bring beauty to them. Since my name has always been something I've struggled with, and for 48 years was called Katie, God reminded me of to whom I belong and my identity. He brought Lasoy from the bottom of the pool, washed my scars, and reminded me of how precious my name is, just like gold.

> *"For we are His workmanship, created in Christ*
> *Jesus for good works, which God prepared*
> *beforehand that we should walk in them."*
> ~ Ephesians 2:10

Following my baptism at Rock Creek Church, I wish I could say things became easier, but things would become harder and different. The way I saw God and life was changing me. Part of the change was shedding people who were not good for me and would keep me stuck in my old behavior and insecurities. In addition, I encountered different sets of arrows and whispers from the enemy. However, this time, I would have someone in my corner and the understanding of who God says I am.

Trusting in the Lord's guidance, I was determined to explore every historical fact about Jesus' life, his followers, and the stories within the Bible. If my relationship with God was real, I wanted to know the real God, from His language and historical aspects. I wanted to be able to say my experience was not for nothing and be able to proudly defend my journey of redemption with a real God because my scars are real.

As I was learning more about the Word of God, He, too, was working behind the scenes to bring me deeper connections with other Christians. As I allowed God to work in me, He allowed me to see the difference of having a deeper connection with fellow sisters in Christ. He changed what I thought a deep connection meant. Before, I thought I needed friends who looked like me, spoke the same language, and ate the same food. Those types of friendships, based on outward appearances, lacked a deeper connection in faith. God allowed me to go through the lessons of what it looks like to have friendships that were of the world versus friends in Christ. God was cleaning my closet, whether I wanted it or not, which included other Christians who played a part in my walk of faith.

If my relationship with God was real, I wanted to know the real God, from His language, and historical aspects.

As my understanding of God's Words deepened, my obedience deepened even further. I trusted God in where to go, who to keep in my close circle, and who I needed to release to grow my faith. While I understood none of it, I trusted Him. I could see things change within our family, as well. I could see how both Van and I softened, and my relationship, especially with my daughter Isabella, grew even deeper. When she was fourteen, I thought aliens kidnapped my sweet daughter and replaced her with a crazy alien full of sass! While Van had his issues with religion, he supported my walk of faith and wanting to know God better. This didn't mean everything was perfect, but it meant the way I handled things was different, my tone was softer, my patience was longer, and I knew how to set better boundaries.

chapter

17

DON'T RIDE THAT SAIL

"But the Lord said to Samuel, 'Do not look on his appearance or on the height of his stature, because I have rejected him. For the Lord sees not as man sees: man looks on the outward appearance, but the Lord looks on the heart.'"

~ 1 Samuel 16:7

During this time, I learned to set boundaries and what it meant to have an authentic relationship with God. While God brought a Christian to help me with my faith, He, too, would use the same Christian to help me realize not to ride the sails of other people's faith.

When I first started my Christian walk, I leaned on one Christian friend for a better understanding of the Bible. As I grew in God's Word and my discernment skills were sharpened, I pushed back and questioned her judgment of others and the things she said versus the things she did. Though I hadn't been a Christian very long, I knew I needed to let the friendship go, but I had so much guilt in letting it go. How could I release a relationship that had grown me closer to God? I thought I was being a good friend by listening to her teach me her thoughts on what the Bible said, but I was riding the sails of her faith rather than developing a unique faith of my own. I had tried to hang on to something that wasn't meant for me, and it brought lots of restless nights. Letting go of that friendship was extremely hard, and I had to grow in my own faith journey, not hers. Some of the things she said and did were hurtful, they reminded me of Christians I knew in high school, where they said one thing and did the other. God would remind me to forgive and release. He would bring the friendships I needed and deepen the ones I currently had, and some friendships were meant for a season to teach us a lesson.

Do not ride the sails of other people's faith.

So, I let go of that friendship and started new sails of my own, allowing God's breath to push it forward. Once I had freed myself from that relationship, I developed a deeper one-on-one time with God each morning. I started journaling scriptures and purchased more books. Even my Amazon Prime video selections changed and became more faith-based and included collections of Bible stories. I'm sure Van thought he was at church service when he clicked on my Amazon account.

While God removed some, He also brought other healthy Christians into my life, and I began to work on my current friendships within my Asian group. While my Asian friends and I had great connections, God caused us to realize that it was not about what was on the outside or the food we ate. He wanted to deepen our relationship and conversation through our faith and the relationship each of us had with God. We started talking about how each of us came to America and how we were all affected or influenced by the generosity of Christian missionaries.

As each morning came, I looked forward to reading my Bible and writing scripture in my journal, and my alone time to talk to God about what was heavy, or the silly things on my mind. Still, each day was hard. I asked God for wisdom and strength to be faithful and trust Him, even when I didn't understand things. He knew there was one area I had to face and completely release myself from. It was my sponsor family and the lost journals and photos from the attic. This was something I did not want to confront or acknowledge. But He reminded me that, this time, I would not be alone in the attic. This time, He would be in the discussion of my lost journals and pictures. I would have someone in my corner guiding me.

It took the world standing still in lockdown for me to revisit that little girl who cried in the attic for her lost items, her beloved journals and photos. Ivy's health started deteriorating and we had reconnected our relationship. I accepted her for loving me in the way she could. No more, no less. She may not have loved me the way I wanted, but it was love, nonetheless.

While my relationship with Ivy was on the mend, my relationship with the sponsor sisters was far from being reconciled. I would learn and hear things being said behind my back. I had started setting boundaries and letting my voice be heard to push back, something they didn't like. Jezel became Ivy's primary caretaker and, as Ivy's health got worse, I couldn't go visit her because of lockdowns. I realized my relationship with Jezel was not going to change. She had her experience, and I had mine. Even at the end of Ivy's life, Jezel was bitter. Like the saying says, hurt people hurt people. We exhausted our text exchange about Ivy, and I no longer wanted to engage with Jezel. I was not going to allow her to make me feel less-than and a charity case they took in. This time, I didn't owe anything to them in the name of acceptance.

Or so I thought. I didn't realize the extent to which Jezel would take things. Months passed and my phone calls to Ivy went unanswered. I would get updates from time to time from Ivy's sister. Then one day, I received a call from my sponsor cousin informing me that Ivy had passed away. The cousin assumed I knew since it had been days since her passing. I was devastated and mourned her loss. However, I couldn't believe I wasn't given a courtesy phone call or text to let me know. That stung and brought me back to the feeling of that little girl who felt like trash when all her things were thrown away. I had lost hope of any of my items surviving at Ivy's house. I had to let go of the thought of ever getting my childhood photos and my beloved journals back.

After Ivy's passing, I discovered they put her house up for sale. While I had given up the thought that any of my belongings had survived, in the bottom of my heart there was a tiny flicker of hope that perhaps something had survived, anything. Van came home to discover my sadness and asked what was wrong, I mentioned to him about the house being sold and the tiny hope that something of mine had indeed survived was dashed away. Days later, Van sat me down and said, "Okay, don't be mad at me, but I did something as a loving husband." With my head tilted and the look of "Oh boy, what on earth did you do?" he began to tell me how he attempted to be reasonable with Jezel to see if anything had remained in the house. One of Van's gifts from God is the ability to read people and know if they are telling the truth.

In so many words, he said -- while hugging me --Jezel was crazy and if he had known the house was for sale, he would have purchased it and we would tear it down, brick by brick, to see if any of my belongings had survived. He proceeded to say Jezel knew about getting rid of my things and tried to cover it up, based on their conversation. I told him that, while I appreciated it, I just wanted to move on with our lives without them in it and to enjoy what God was building. I didn't need those journals or photos; I had everything I could ever hope for – my journals were our children. My journals would live on through our children and they, too, would make other wonderful stories of their own.

While I said those things out loud, God knew the longing inside my heart. Within months, I was introduced to a photographer, her information was inside a booklet left by a friend inside my mailbox as a gift. Her name was MeRa Koh, and she did something called the *Rising Phoenix Experience,* where people would fly in from around the country to experience its powerful healing. MeRa Koh and her team combine neuroscience with photography to help heal the brain, mind, and spirit. Through phone calls with people and their loved ones, MeRa's team would identify key attributes of others' resilience to capture their beauty from within, to remind them of their true selves daily.

I didn't exactly know what I was getting myself into. I thought it would be nice to have a photography experience, maybe it would help, maybe it wouldn't. All I knew was that perhaps it was time to let my guard down and trust the process of taking photos with my scars.

When MeRa reached out to me, we shared each other's life experiences, and we immediately bonded. There in her studio, I began the process of having photos taken of my scars. God needed me to let go of the photos in the attic to give me beautiful, redeemed photos I was meant to have. MeRa captured the beauty of every scar. After seeing the photos, there were no words, just tears. My photos were not lost; they were found and made new.

For the first time, I saw how God made each scar beautiful with its own story. The journey of their redemption. Each scar told stories. Not stories of rejection but of acceptance. Not of brokenness but of strength. Not of sorrow but of joy. My photos from MeRa were indeed the process of Kintsugi, rejoining with gold what had been broken, making it more valuable.

No longer were my photos lost. They were found and made new with beauty. Seeing myself in a new light allowed me to see my journey from the East to the West as redemption. Not only for myself but also for others. With a better understanding of grace and forgiveness of others who have hurt me, as found in Romans 12, I learned to let go so that God could transform me into His identity.

This transformation opened me to new and healthier relationships in my life.

chapter

18

DEEPER JOY

Since I wanted nothing to do with God for most of my life and had turned away from anything concerning Christianity, there was a lot to catch up on. It was as though I was in ESL, this time with God guiding my steps. I had to retrain my mind and wash away the things the world had taught about what the Bible said and what it meant to be a faithful Christian. I found deep joy and a deeper peace in my walk with the Lord, learning that it has nothing to do with religion and everything to do with an authentic relationship with God. I didn't have to earn His love; it is freely given. It was a big revelation and an even bigger relief, knowing that my imperfections didn't matter. Some of the joys I found were an almost childlike wonder.

I've heard that God has a funny sense of humor; little did I know how big His humor is. For so many years, I kept away from Jesus' people. Then I became the very people I tried to get away from.

This part of my journey makes me laugh with complete joy in my discovery of what Jesus people say. Perhaps one day I will create a compilation book called *Christian Lingo for Dummies*. As I was going through my walk of faith, God brought other Christian friends to help me navigate Christian terms and lingo.

Once I became involved with other Christian activities, I would listen to their conversations and pick up on words and phrases that made me feel like a deer in the headlights. Thank goodness God brought godly females who would answer my questions without fear of being mocked. I was safe with them in asking silly to tough questions about the Bible.

I remember my first encounter with the Christian terms, "seasons and equally yoked." It was at my first Bible study on Joseph's journey. One of the ladies was talking about the difficult "season" she was in and how she was thankful for being "equally yoked." I looked across the room thinking to myself, *what the heck is she talking about?* As far as I knew there are only four seasons. Do these Jesus people have more than four seasons? Are they going to be chasing me down and breaking an egg on my head so I could be covered with the yolk?

Yes, as silly as that may sound, those were questions

I wasn't quite sure of. Later my friend Jill explained what being *equally yoked* meant in scripture. That was a big relief. Then, the things Pastor Brad spoke about made more sense.

Later I discovered and attended my first revival when MeRa asked if I would like to join her. Before my baptism, I thought revivals consisted of big white tents, banjos, and snakes. When MeRa asked me to attend a revival, I was hesitant. But because I cherished our friendship, I was willing to take the risk of snakes. I asked MeRa what type of shoes she would wear when they passed out the snakes. She laughed and assured me there would not be snakes or banjos, and the event would be held inside. Tears of laughter streamed down our faces, and what a relief that MeRa took the time to explain what an actual revival is. In my mind, I had envisioned Jesus people sweating outside with weird banjo music while passing out snakes. It was hilarious. But as a precaution, I wore sneakers and scoured the parking lot for white tents.

Once inside her church, the place was filled with people singing and praising God. The music was electrifying with people moving, clapping, dancing, and rejoicing to God. It was amazing, and I was relieved I was going home with hope instead of with snakes.

There would be plenty more of those types of laughter with the new friendships I formed with my circle of Christian friends. They were not judgy, stuffy Christians with no sense of humor that I thought they would be. They were welcoming, funny, and made learning about the

Word of God normal and relatable. I was able to let my guard down with them about God.

When praying for Christian friends, I would ask God to please bring me godly ladies but please don't make them weird, and mostly, don't make me weird around them. God gave me some of the most incredible ladies in my life. They were prayer warriors, encouragers, and brought the best out of me during my worst days. I'm proud to lay my life down for them. They were the type of sisters I've always wanted, encouragers and funny at the same time. I am finally at peace with the right kind of friendships: godly friendships with joy.

> When praying for Christian friends, I would ask God to please bring me godly ladies but please don't make them weird, and mostly, don't make me weird around them.

That type of joy and peace came full circle when I was asked to serve on the board for two organizations. God knew that I wanted to help others who were struggling at the crossroads of their journey. Everyone deserves to be seen and a second chance to restore their dignity and life.

Today, I sit on the board of an organization called Treasured Vessels Foundation which helps the recovery process of victims of sex trafficking. It serves as a reminder that the root cause of sex trafficking is human exploitation. Both my mother and sister didn't have the luxury of love, they had to forgo love to survive. Bounmy was exploited and made to work two jobs and hand her paycheck over without the ability to read or write in Thai. I think about what both their lives would have been like if there was an origination like TVF, that allowed them to recover and have a second chance to rebuild their lives. To be seen and a safe place to rest their heads.

The other organization is the Foundation for CHOICE (Consider How One Individual Changes Everything), helping low-income students break the cycle of poverty through higher education. God taught me, someone who had struggled financially to attend college and didn't have a mother or mentor, to help students in an at-risk neighborhood navigate their high school and college life. At FFC, I am both a board member and mentor for students to help them finish high school and attend college. I could relate to the students about their struggles of attending college, since I had been in their shoes, because of my financial circumstances. When I worked odd jobs to put myself through college, I worked for a boss who used my youth and naivety to force me to perform tasks I was not qualified for. Through that situation, God taught me how to help students stand up and find their voices when they are caught in situations where adults in a position of power or authority try to coerce them into doing something against their will. To help even one student see their potential and help them shine makes everything I've been through worth it.

God went even further to use our children, whom I did not raise in church but wanted them to find their unique relationship with Him. Kohl now serves as a youth pastor. Patrick continues to grow his faith to share his strength and kindness with those around him, and Isabella is growing in her faith while attending a local church near her college campus and serving. Indeed, God has a funny sense of humor to use our children to lead others to Christ, making them part of the Jesus people I once wanted to avoid.

Most importantly, God is in the business of redemption, taking someone like me who grew up without a mother, someone with deep insecurities in motherhood, who has been chasing a mother figure her entire life. God made me look within to be the mother I always wanted, not only for our children but for others, as well.

Our mother, Dy, wanted our voices to live on and was willing to pay the ultimate price so we could make it to America. I want our voices to live on and honor God, thus I created our foundation, Community 75. I think our mother wanted us to have a family and community to help everyone feel loved, seen, and not defined by their circumstances and hardships. Like the time I didn't have seventy-five dollars, it's a reminder that in my suffering, God saw me and was with me during my darkest moment. He didn't need me; He wanted me. Those times He was by my side, wiping my tears away, not one of them was wasted.

When there's deep sorrow, God brings deeper joy. Though my body is riddled with scars, not one of my bones has been broken. It's a testament to God's faithfulness. Not just for myself, but for others, as well.

Whether you're currently searching for redemption, in the process of redemption, or have experienced God's mercy of redemption, just hold on. Your journey is yet to be completed.

"The Lord is close to the brokenhearted and rescues those whose spirits are crushed. The righteous person faces many troubles, but the Lord comes to the rescue each time. For the Lord protects the bones of the righteous; not one of them is broken!"
~ Psalm 34:18-20

CONCLUSION

"Then Jesus said to those Jews who believed Him, 'If you abide in My word, you are My disciples indeed. And you shall know the truth, and the truth shall make you free.'"
~ John 8:31-32

May the discomfort of our scars always remind us of Whom we belong to. We are uniquely created by God for His purpose as stated in Genesis 1:2. A friend once said that there are two significant dates in our lives: the day we are born and the day we discover our purpose. Although my purpose is marked by visible scars, from my face to my finger and down to my stomach, it has been a challenging yet fulfilling journey.

God has called all of us, the broken but undefeated, for such a time as this, to lean on Him and help others heal by lighting their steps back to our true home. I think this is part of His great commission.

Writing this book was not my initial desire, but it is my

calling. It means revisiting my wounds, exposing my deepest fears and insecurities, and reliving the tough lessons I've learned. However, God has called all of us, the broken but undefeated, for such a time as this, to lean on Him and help others heal by lighting their steps back to our true home through our testimony. I think this is part of His great commission.

God never said our time on Earth would be easy, and that our testimony wouldn't be painful. He has reminded me why we must press forward and that it isn't for nothing. Revelation 12:11 says, *"They triumphed over him by the blood of the Lamb and by the word of their testimony."* Testimonies have power; they remind us of God's faithfulness in His ability to heal, restore, and redeem. It is a weapon of encouragement.

The truth about our lives is raw, unfiltered, and painfully universal. Life doesn't stop when we are exhausted, broken, when our hearts are shattered, or when our spirits feel broken. It keeps moving, unyielding, and indifferent while demanding that we keep pace. There is no pause button for grief, no intermission for healing, no moment where the world gently steps aside and allows us to mend. Life expects us to carry our burdens in silence and to push forward despite the weight of all we carry inside.

The cruelest part? We may gain some perspective through others' defeats and triumphs, but no one prepares us for this. As children, we are fed stories of resilience wrapped in neat, hopeful fairytale endings where pain has a purpose, and every storm clears to reveal a bright rainbow horizon. But adulthood strips away those comforting illusions. It teaches us that survival is rarely poetic like children raising children.

More often than not, it's about showing up when we'd rather disappear, smiling through pain no one sees, and carrying on despite feeling like we're unraveling from the inside out. And yet, somehow, we persevere. That's the quiet miracle of being human. Even when life is relentless, even when hope feels distant, we keep moving. We stumble, we break, we fall to our knees, but we get up. And in doing so, we uncover a strength, when we learn to trust in God, that He makes a way when there is no way.

Sometimes in our darkest moments and weakness, we ask God, "Why?" I found my answer in Romans 8:28 *"And we know that all things work together for good to those who love God, to those who are called according to His purpose."*

Sometimes the Lord takes away so He can teach us to surrender. Sometimes He allows heartbreak so that He can heal us. Sometimes He doesn't give the answer right away, so we learn to trust Him. Sometimes He reminds us how weak we are so that we remember how strong He is.

Slowly, we realize that resilience isn't always about grand acts of bravery or being the smartest person in the room. Sometimes, it's just a whisper from God telling us to "Keep going." It's the willingness to take that leap of faith. Yes, it's exhausting. Yes, it's unfair. And yes, there are days when the weight of it all feels unbearable and we're hanging on by a thread, drowning. But every small step in trusting God is a step forward, it is proof that we haven't given up and the water will not overtake us. That we are still fighting, still holding on, still refusing to let the darkness consume us. That quiet defiance of choosing to exist, to try, to hope, is the bravest thing we can do. There is a loving purpose in everything He does, even when we don't know "the why."

"O give thanks unto the Lord, for He is good: for His mercy endureth forever. Let the redeemed of the Lord say so, whom He hath redeemed from the hand of the enemy; And gathered them out of the lands, from the East, and from the West, from the North, and from the South."
~ Psalm 107:1-3

God's love for us is unwavering, and He works tirelessly to ensure a bright future for us all. When we release the pain, hurt, and negative self-perceptions, we can embrace the truth of how cherished we are in God's eyes. Each day, upon waking, imagine how different you would feel knowing that you are deeply valued by God and that your worth is not determined by your performance, or lack thereof. God loves you simply for being you, we are His workmanship.

What if everything we have been through is preparing us for everything we've been asking for? Allow God to bring beauty from your pain. It's never wasted, but it's transformed for your redemption story.

"Blessed are ye that hunger now: for ye shall be filled.
Blessed are ye that weep now: for ye shall laugh."
~ Luke 6:21

Where there is deep sorrow is an even deeper joy. Amen.

ABOUT THE AUTHOR

Lasoy Katie Singleton is a passionate advocate for social impact, and a dedicated wife and mother. As a first-generation immigrant and the first in her family to graduate from both high school and college, Katie has achieved remarkable success as one of the few female Development Managers at Microsoft. Her expertise encompasses software development, including innovations such as personal digital assistants (PDAs).

In addition, Katie is an active board member for two impactful organizations: Treasured Vessels Foundation (TVF) and Foundation For CHOICE (FFC). At TVF, she fervently supports the mission to aid survivors of human trafficking. Through her leadership with FFC, Katie takes great pride in mentoring high school students, providing them with invaluable guidance as they navigate their educational and career paths.

Married to her husband Van for 24 years, Katie is a devoted wife and mother to three wonderful children, all while managing a lively household that includes seven dogs. Her strong Christian faith inspired her to establish a personal foundation called Community 75, which is dedicated to uplifting organizations and individuals in their pursuit of purpose. Additionally, Katie leads a life group known as the Sisterhood of Swans, fostering supportive, faith-based friendships among women.